Can we afford the future?

THE NEW ECONOMICS

Economics is changing fast. Important recent research in heterodox traditions has shed light on some of the world's most intractable problems, challenging the old ways of doing things and rendering economics more human and more real.

The New Economics shows how economics can be used in novel and creative ways, to resolve issues and improve conditions, not just entrench the way things are. Covering topics as diverse as climate change, inequality, gender, global institutions and development, these books offer new perspectives on the pressing issues of our time.

Short, argumentative and accessible, the books are essential reading for a new generation of students, activists and policymakers, as well as for people who just want to know more.

The New Economics is edited by three internationally renowned economists: Bina Agarwal at the Institute of Economic Growth in India; Ha-Joon Chang at the University of Cambridge in the UK, and Kevin Gallagher at Boston University in the USA.

Can we afford the future?

The economics of a warming world

FRANK ACKERMAN

ZED BOOKS
London & New York

Can We Afford the Future? The Economics of a Warming World
was first published in 2009 by Zed Books Ltd, 7 Cynthia Street, London
N1 9JF, UK and Room 400, 175 Fifth Avenue, New York, NY 10010, USA

www.zedbooks.co.uk

Designed and typeset in Monotype Ehrhardt
by illuminati, www.illuminatibooks.co.uk
Cover designed by Rogue Four Design
Printed and bound in the UK by CPI Antony Rowe,
Chippenham, Wiltshire

Distributed in the USA exclusively by Palgrave Macmillan, a division
of St Martin's Press, LLC, 175 Fifth Avenue, New York, NY 10010

A catalogue record for this book is available from the British Library
Library of Congress Cataloging in Publication Data available

ISBN   978 1 84813 037 1 hb
ISBN   978 1 84813 038 8 pb

Contents

Acknowledgements

Although none of them shares the responsibility for anything
that is wrong or annoying, many people provided suggestions
and comments which I relied on in writing this book. My col-
league Elizabeth A. Stanton, who read and commented on the
manuscript, is my co-author on a number of recent publications
on climate change, which I have drawn on in many places. Lisa
Heinzerling, my co-author on critiques of cost–benefit analysis,
also made helpful comments; much of Chapter 1 is drawn from
an article by Lisa and me, "Law and Economics for a Warming
World." Cornelia Herzfeld commented on the text throughout
– and took on the job of making the manuscript more presentable,
grammatical, and book-like in appearance. Neva Goodwin, Julie
Nelson, and Martin Weitzman also provided valuable comments
on early drafts. Conversations with Sivan Kartha and Paul Baer
helped me write Chapter 8. A discussion with Steve DeCanio
suggested the opening contrast of climate change to an anticipated

asteroid impact, though, again, Steve is not responsible for what I did with his provocative idea.

Many chapters draw on my previous work, as indicated in the notes and bibliography. In particular, Chapter 6 is a shortened form of my review of the Stern Review and subsequent debate, written for Friends of the Earth, and Chapter 7 is a shortened form of my review of Bjørn Lomborg's *Cool It*, which appeared in *Climatic Change*. Thanks to Simon Bullock at Friends of the Earth and to Stephen Schneider at *Climatic Change* for encouraging and publishing these reviews.

Thanks to Kevin Gallagher for suggesting that I write this book, to Kevin and his co-editors Ha-Joon Chang and Bina Agarwal for inviting me to be the first in their new book series, and to Ellen McKinlay at Zed Books for moving this project forward so smoothly. Support from the Rockefeller Brothers Fund and from the Stockholm Environment Institute was crucial to the process of writing.

Thanks to Becky Sarah for her thoughts about grandparenting, which may have influenced Chapter 2 – and for everything else.

I

The status quo is not an option

NEW YORK   NASA scientists today confirmed that a massive
asteroid is headed for a collision with the Earth a few years from
now. The impact will make our planet largely uninhabitable,
killing most of the human race and causing the extinction of
most species. There is barely enough time to build the rockets
needed to deflect the asteroid and prevent a global catastrophe.

Fictional news items along those lines have been imagined often
enough, in disaster movies and pulp fiction. The exact response
to the warning varies, as does the ultimate outcome. But no one
ever suggests waiting for the outcome of a cost–benefit analysis to
determine whether or not it is worthwhile to build the rockets and
save the planet.

This is not a book about asteroids and disaster movies. Rather,
it is about another global catastrophe that is on a collision course
with our future: the threat of climate change. According to real
scientists at NASA and elsewhere, there is a real risk that climate

change could make the planet largely uninhabitable for people and for most other species. And there is – just barely – enough time to avert the disaster.

Yet when it comes to global warming, the wisdom shown in disaster movies is often lacking. Many people worry that climate policy could be ruinously expensive; in this view, it is essential to begin with detailed economic analysis, and to ensure that we move cautiously and avoid excessive expenditure. That is, perhaps we should begin with a cost–benefit calculation to find out how much prevention of climate catastrophe we can afford to "buy." All too often, the answer has been that we should do relatively little for now.

For example, Yale economist William Nordhaus, the economist best known for his work on climate change, pays lip service to scientists' calls for decisive action. He finds, however, that the "optimal" policy is a very small carbon tax that would reduce greenhouse gas emissions only 25 percent below "business-as-usual" levels by 2050 – in other words, allowing emissions to rise well above current levels by mid-century.[1] (In contrast, several European governments and US states have called for reductions of 50 percent to 80 percent below 1990 levels by 2050.)

A number of economists have criticized the Kyoto Protocol – the international agreement, ratified by all industrial countries except the US, which called for a first, modest round of emissions reductions by 2012. Yale economist Sheila Olmstead and Harvard economist Robert Stavins deem the Kyoto Protocol "deeply flawed" and recommend instead that we allow emissions to rise for a few decades before requiring any reductions.[2]

And economists have lobbied and spoken against other small, initial steps toward emissions reduction. A group of well-known economists, including Robert Hahn of AEI–Brookings and Paul Joskow and Richard Schmalensee of MIT, filed a legal brief before the US Supreme Court opposing EPA regulation of carbon dioxide emissions from automobiles. That brief, funded by automobile dealers across the country, claimed that such regulation would be expensive and inefficient.[3]

The economic case for inaction on climate change is not just an obscure academic doctrine. Economists' doubts and conclusions about climate change echo throughout the public debate; economic analysis has a major impact on the decisions that politicians and governments are willing to take. There is much more than economic theory at stake.

This book offers an alternative understanding of climate economics, one that is compatible with the warnings of impending crisis that increasingly emerge from climate science. To preview the story, this chapter begins with a look at the ways in which conventional economics is implicitly, but fundamentally, biased in favor of the status quo.[4] Climate change challenges that bias, since the message of climate science is that the status quo – the current climate – is being undermined, and changed for the worse, by our actions.

The next four chapters examine four key aspects of climate economics. Chapter 2 introduces discounting, a much-debated process that provides a quantitative measure of our relationship and responsibility to future generations. The choice of the discount rate involves ethics and politics, not just economic technicalities; it is a choice that is all-important for the evaluation of climate costs and benefits. Chapter 3 turns to the analysis of risk and uncertainty, suggesting that worst-case outcomes, potentially sufficient to end life as we know it, may now be likely as events that people insure themselves against. Viewing climate policy as insurance leads to a different perspective from cost–benefit analysis, focusing on preventing worst cases rather than calculating average or expected values.

The following two chapters look at the benefits and the costs of climate policy. Chapter 4 explores the priceless nature of the potential health and environmental damages from climate change, along with the strange hypotheses about the benefits of moderate warming that have crept into the economics literature. Chapter 5 examines the costs of climate policy, highlighting the role of economic theory in shaping our understanding and our estimates of those costs, and the factors that promote the development of new technologies.

Economics does not speak with a single voice on climate change. Chapters 6 and 7 review the worst and the best of recent economic perspectives on the problem. Bjørn Lomborg, the Danish political scientist turned anti-environmental gadfly, relies heavily on conventional economic analyses to build his case for doing little if anything about climate change; his writing has received an inordinate amount of media attention. Chapter 6 shows what's wrong with Lomborg, and the economists he quotes in his latest attack on active climate policies. At the other end of the spectrum, the British government asked Nicholas Stern to review the economics of climate change; the resulting Stern Review extended the boundaries of the debate, using standard techniques of cost–benefit analysis to support large-scale emissions reduction initiatives. Chapter 7 argues that the Stern Review is far from perfect, but is much less wrong than other well-known analyses.

The last two chapters take up the questions of climate policy. Climate change is a global problem facing an unequal world; the problem of international equity is central to the issue, as seen in

Chapter 8. Industrial countries not only have much greater per capita carbon emissions; they also have benefited from a history of high carbon emissions and have greater resources than other countries for solving the problem. Is it possible to create a formula for sharing the global economic burden of climate protection, which wins acceptance from all? Finally, Chapter 9 offers economic perspectives on climate policy, including doubts about the potential of some proposed technical fixes, an examination of the role and limitations of market mechanisms, and closing thoughts on the required extent and pace of change.

Much of the error and mischief described in this book rests on standard, abstract economic theory – a subject that may understandably lead some readers to roll their eyes and start flipping the pages. But hang on: there's something in there you need to know, to understand the climate change debate today. The rest of this chapter offers a very quick tour of the biases of conventional economic theory, as seen through the lens of climate change.

The new debate

Once upon a time, debates about climate policy were primarily about the science. Initially, at least in the US, an inordinate amount of attention was focused on the handful of "climate skeptics" who challenged the scientific understanding of climate change. The influence of the skeptics, however, is rapidly fading; few people were swayed by their arguments, and doubt or uncertainty about the major results of climate science is no longer important in shaping public policy.

Many summaries are available of the current understanding of climate science.[5] Briefly, the threat of climate change includes the predictable, gradual increase in average temperatures – and much more. Continuation of current patterns of fossil fuel combustion, deforestation, and other causes of greenhouse gas emissions will, within fifty to a hundred years or less, cause massive melting of glaciers and ice sheets, extinction of many climate-sensitive species, widespread droughts in (at least) South Asia, Africa, and western North America, decline in global food production (even as the world's population grows well beyond today's levels), and more destructive extreme weather events, along the lines of the US hurricanes of 2005 and the European heatwave of 2003. And the news will only grow worse as atmospheric carbon dioxide levels continue to rise.

As the climate *science* debate is reaching closure, the climate *economics* debate is heating up. The controversial issue now is the fear that overly ambitious climate initiatives could hurt the economy. The alleged danger is that we might do "too much" to reduce emissions, resulting in costs that would outweigh some estimates of the benefits. Yet once the question is posed in these terms, a bias toward inaction is already creeping in.

Implicit in the usual framing of a cost–benefit analysis is the notion that, if costs exceed benefits, we can decline to take any new initiative. Doing nothing is the default; there is a higher hurdle for justifying action than for continuing inaction. "Only take action if the benefits exceed the costs" is a superficially plausible rule for making decisions. Yet even when the economic analysis is implemented with generous intent, it still has a built-in bias, via the presumption that the status quo prevails until and unless a policy passes a cost–benefit test.[6]

It is here that climate science and economics appear to clash head-on. The urgency of the climate problem, the ever-increasing scientific certainty that "business as usual" will lead to irreversible, unacceptable outcomes, undermines any presumption in favor of the status quo. What the science tells us, above all, is that the status quo is not going to remain one of the available options.

Suppose that, as in some recent economic analyses, the answer is that we cannot or should not do much about climate change for now. What would it mean to conclude that the costs of avoiding a climate disaster exceed the benefits? Perhaps the future is a high-priced luxury item that we can't quite afford. Rather than investing in a sustainable world for our descendants, should we have one last party and then pull the plug?

We can, in fact, afford to create a livable future, especially if we start immediately; the longer we wait, the more expensive and difficult it will become. We can't afford to spend more time being confused by mistaken theories claiming that the logic of economics somehow calls for gradualism and delay. Thus the creation of a sensible response to climate change requires a look at what's wrong with economic theory. Climate change is not an isolated flaw in an otherwise perfect market system; rather, it is a systemic failure, requiring a new approach. The implicit assumption of a higher burden of proof for those who want change is obsolete if the world is on a collision course with disaster. *Something* new and different has to be done.

Conventional economic theory reflexively shuns intervention in private markets. Economists often view the world in terms of market equilibrium, a state of affairs that cannot be improved upon without hurting someone. Even though few economists would argue that the world currently reflects this utopian ideal, many do assume that we are close enough to it that only small intrusions in the market, in the nature of tidying up rather than major renovations, are required. This theory does not come close to describing the world we live in, and it arises from highly contestable assumptions about the importance of free markets to human freedom.

The invisible hand, and other fables

The customary starting point for economic theory, the basic model to which other situations and policy options are compared, is a system of perfectly competitive markets. This imagined economy is populated exclusively by small producers and individual consumers, all possessed of very broad information and very narrow motives and desires. In such an economy, under long lists of traditional but unrealistic assumptions, economists have proved that there is always an "equilibrium" – that is, a set of prices at which supply equals demand for every commodity. The invisible hand of market competition, in Adam Smith's famous metaphor, ensures that every resource is used wherever it will produce the greatest value for consumers. Any deviation from the free-market outcome will make someone worse off, so there is no possible change to a market equilibrium that could win unanimous support.

In this model economy, environmental problems appear only as an afterthought, in the form of "externalities": unpriced damages imposed by one party on another. Externalities, it is assumed, can be given prices and incorporated into the calculations of the marketplace, whether through taxes, negotiations, or the invention of markets for pollution rights. With externalities correctly priced, the optimal properties of market equilibrium are restored.

No one, presumably, views this as an accurate description of any large part of our twenty-first-century world. For some economists, the optimality of an abstract, perfectly competitive market economy is an ideal worth striving toward. More common is the claim that this apparatus is analytically useful: the implications of the perfect-market model can be worked out with mathematical precision, and then reality can be understood in terms of its (minor) deviations from the model.

The centrality of equilibrium to economics is emphasized by a leading textbook on microeconomic theory:

> A characteristic feature that distinguishes economics from other scientific fields is that, for us, the equations of equilibrium constitute the center of our discipline. Other sciences, such as physics or even ecology, put comparatively more emphasis on the determination of dynamic laws of change.[7]

Ironically, the "equations of equilibrium" in economics arise from models borrowed from the physical sciences of the nineteenth century.[8] The theoretical equilibrium of a system of perfect markets bears more than a passing resemblance to the theory of an ideal gas, which you may have encountered in a physics class. In the course of the twentieth century, economics developed intricately mathematical versions of this classic theory of equilibrium. At the same time, the physical sciences moved on to extend and modify their nineteenth-century equilibrium models, developing subtle and powerful analyses of complex, potentially chaotic systems, such as the earth's climate, where disequilibrium can easily arise.

The greater commitment to equilibrium theories in economics may reflect the political significance of the subject matter. Thermodynamic equilibrium and disequilibrium are states of nature, with, presumably, the same neutral, apolitical meaning to physicists of widely varying political views. In contrast, the market equilibrium of economic theory maximizes efficiency, a desirable social goal. It has become bound up with advocacy of laissez-faire policies, seen by some as the route to political as well as economic freedom. In the words of the influential conservative economist Milton Friedman, "[T]he central feature of the market organization of economic activity is that it prevents one person from interfering with another in respect of most of his activities. ... Underlying most arguments against the free market is a lack of belief in freedom itself."[9]

There are at least two problems with Friedman's claim. First, the theoretical realm of perfect markets, with every industry made up exclusively of small, competitive businesses, bears little resemblance to the reality of Microsoft in software, Wal-Mart in retailing, Boeing and Airbus in airplane production, and the giant corporations that dominate the media, finance, and many other fields. Replacing them all with numerous small, competitive firms is clearly out of the question.

Advocates of laissez-faire, like Friedman, tend to take it for granted that any movement toward an unregulated competitive market is desirable, since it brings the real world closer to the ideal. However, the "theory of the second best," developed long ago by Richard Lipsey and Kelvin Lancaster, proves that if one of the requirements for an ideal outcome cannot be achieved, the best attainable (or "second best") outcome may require a major deviation from the ideal.[10] Informally, if the fastest route for driving through a city is blocked by construction, the next-fastest option may involve a completely different main road, not the side streets that stay as close as possible to the preferred route. The theory of the second best undermines the significance of the competitive market model as a goal; if the goal is not, in its entirety, attainable, there is no guarantee that getting a little closer to it is on balance a good thing.

Second, Friedman's vision is of a world without important externalities: in his view, the normal operation of the market "prevents one person from interfering with another" in most of life's activities. The climate crisis, however, implies that market activities and the resulting greenhouse gas emissions are going to interfere on a grand scale with other people's lives. This is not a single, easily internalized externality; rather, climate change is a pervasive consequence of modern market activity, which ultimately threatens to undermine the continued existence of the market economy itself.

Economics without equilibrium

There have been economic theories that assumed a world in disequilibrium – or that at least did not assume competitive equilibrium governed by an all-powerful invisible hand. The macroeconomics of John Maynard Keynes, developed to explain the widespread, persistent unemployment and depression of the 1930s, is one of the best-known examples. Keynes's theories assumed that businesses and investors will make repeated errors in judgment, and implied that the economy could be stuck for a while at a high rate of unemployment. However, Keynes ultimately offered an optimistic outlook, suggesting that better judgment and skillful government policy could restore full employment and economic growth. In contrast, the climate crisis paints a darker picture, implying that normal market activity will undermine its own continuation.

A deeper sense of internal contradiction and instability was present in two distinct branches of nineteenth-century political economy, in the writings of Marx and of Malthus. For Marx, instability arose from the nature of the relationship between capital and labor, a perspective that is not directly relevant here. Malthus was one step closer to the broad outlines of the climate problem; he was describing a way in which market activity would inevitably lead to environmental degradation, and thus to loss of incomes. However, the logic of Malthusian crisis – prosperity leads to population growth and rising demand for food, which eventually overwhelms the naturally limited productivity of agriculture – does not correspond closely to the major causal mechanisms of climate crisis. Something akin to the Malthusian crisis may be one of the consequences of climate change, as global warming is expected to reduce agricultural productivity relatively soon in the tropics, and perhaps after a few decades in temperate zones – but this is only part of a broader problem.

Natural constraints on economic growth have been raised more recently in ecological economics. This school of thought, drawing on the work of Herman Daly and others, has emphasized that the economy is embedded in the earth's ecosystems, which impose fixed limits on the sustainable scale of production and emissions. While this represents a promising contribution with obvious relevance to climate change, ecological economics does not yet offer a complete theory of economics and the environment – and it has not had much influence on the economics profession in general.

The challenge of climate change makes the traditional vision of perfect markets even less appropriate. A world in which business as usual threatens to cause disaster in less than a century is not usefully modeled by theories in which stable, optimal equilibrium is the norm. Yet the notion that the market economy is or could easily be at equilibrium continues to permeate economic theory; market equilibrium is generally taken to be desirable, and implicitly assumed to be sustainable. If conventional theories of optimal market outcomes encourage a public policy of inaction on climate change, these theories may ironically hasten the arrival of a de-cidedly suboptimal, disequilibrium state of affairs.

Four bumper stickers for better economics

The complexity of the theories under discussion here may seem intimidating. But the point is not that everyone needs to explore the deepest details of economic calculations and theories. The economists who are criticized in these pages, along with those who are praised, are generally very good at the details; their spreadsheets and computer models lead to quite logical conclusions. If, that is, you accept their assumptions. The goal here is to identify the mistaken assumptions that lead smart people to reach such wrong conclusions.

The issues at stake are too important to be left to specialists; they influence public policy choices on the decisive environmental question affecting the fate of the earth. There is a need to open up public understanding and debate on the controversial, underlying assumptions. To that end, the key ideas have to be extracted from the theoretical debates and expressed in simple, transparent form – ideally, in a form suitable for printing on bumper stickers.

Here are the bumper stickers for the four crucial ideas about climate economics, the correctives to the complacent theories of equilibrium and inaction:

Your grandchildren's lives are important

We need to buy insurance for the planet

Climate damages are too valuable to have prices

Some costs are better than others

The next four chapters explain the stories behind the bumper stickers. Together, they form the basis for an improved economics of climate change, one that eliminates the bias toward inaction and endorses prompt, vigorous efforts to reduce carbon emissions. The final four chapters explore the use of these ideas, in making sense of the complex debate about climate economics.

2

Your grandchildren's lives are important

When your grandchildren are the same age as you are today, what will their lives be like? And what is it worth spending today, to improve their future lives – or at least to avoid damaging their prospects? This chapter inescapably involves some thinking about arithmetic, but it's really about how we decide what we will leave to our grandchildren.

Climate change is a long-term problem, spanning more than one generation. Carbon dioxide, the most important greenhouse gas, stays in the atmosphere and continues to heat up the earth for a century or more after it is emitted. Even if nothing else goes wrong, the warming of the atmosphere that we have already caused will continue to heat up the depths of the oceans for several centuries – causing an ongoing rise in sea levels as all that water warms and expands.

The most widely debated challenge of climate economics is the valuation of the very long run. The time spans involved are well beyond those encountered in most areas of economics. For ordinary investments, both the costs today and the resulting future benefits typically occur within a single lifetime. Home mortgages, the longest-lasting financial contracts that most people ever sign, rarely extend beyond 30 years. In such cases, it makes sense to think in terms of the same person experiencing and comparing the costs and the benefits.

On the very different time scale of climate change, 30 years is the short run. Much of the climate damages that will occur over the next 30 years are already locked in, the results of past emissions that can no longer be changed. It is common for climate models to look ahead 100 years or more – in other words, to project the impacts of today's climate choices on generations to come, long after all of us making those choices have passed away. As a result, the costs of reducing emissions today, and the benefits in the far future, will not be experienced by the same people. The economics of climate change is centrally concerned with our relationship to our descendants whom we will never meet.

As a bridge to those unknowable future generations, consider your grandchildren. They are the last generation that most of us will know; indeed, we will be lucky to witness much, if any, of their adult lives. To make the story more specific, assume that your grandchildren will reach your present age, on average, 60 years from now.

What kind of money will your grandchildren be spending 60 years from now? It may still be called dollars,* but they will not be the same dollars you are spending today. Inflation may reduce the value of the dollar, of course, but that is not the point of this

---

* Everything discussed here works equally well with pounds, euros, or any other currency.

story. To look beyond the effects of inflation, let's express all future costs and benefits in terms of the amount they could purchase at today's prices. If we expect 5 percent inflation next year, then $105 at next year's prices has the same purchasing power as $100 at today's prices; so we can refer to it as $100 in "real" or inflation-adjusted dollars.

Suppose that your goal is to leave money to your grandchildren. Which is worth more to them: setting aside $100 for them today, or giving them $100 in the future? They are clearly better off if you set aside the money today. If you put it in a bank account that paid 3 percent annual interest and left it there for 60 years, then thanks to compound interest, your grandchildren would receive $589.

Alternatively, if your goal was to leave your grandchildren with $100, you could put just $17 in the bank for 60 years at 3 percent, and they would end up with $100. In the jargon of economics, this can be expressed by saying that $17 today is the *present value* of $100 to be received (or paid) 60 years from now, at a *discount rate* of 3 percent. That is, the present value is the amount you would have to put in a bank account today, earning interest at discount rate, to end up with the target amount at the specified time in the future.[1]

When economists want to compare dollars paid and received in different years, this is the logic they use. In our example, $100 received by your grandchildren 60 years from now has a present value of $17. A smaller amount, $41, received 30 years from now has the same present value; that's what you would get if you put $17 in the bank and waited only 30 years before withdrawing it (continuing the assumption of 3 percent interest). So, at a 3 percent discount rate, both $100 received 60 years from now, and $41 received 30 years from now, have the same present value as $17 today.[2]

For private financial decisions that involve events within a single lifetime, discounting and calculations of present value are undeniably useful. Suppose that you are considering an investment today with predictable returns in the future. If the present value of those returns exceeds the cost of the investment, it is a better deal than leaving the money in the bank. If the present value of the returns is less than the cost, you are better off sticking with the bank account.

From the other side, if you have borrowed money for a school loan, car loan, or home mortgage, you have undoubtedly noticed that the sum of the payments is much greater than the amount you borrowed. What you are paying for is the use of the money for a period of time. Express the payments as present values, using the interest rate on the loan as the discount rate, and you will find that the present value of all the payments together equals the amount you borrowed.

Discounting the far future

What happens when we apply the logic of discounting to the long-term decisions involved in climate change policy? Climate costs and benefits occur at many different times in the future; discounting provides a ready-made formula for comparing them. Economic analyses of climate change typically apply discounting to convert dollar amounts in widely separated years into directly comparable, present value terms.

The result is that the choice of the discount rate becomes decisive for the whole analysis. It is not an exaggeration to say that the discount rate is the most important single number in climate economics. What look like small differences in discount rates can have huge effects on present values, with the effects growing larger as we look farther into the future. As we will see, a low discount rate makes the future more important, and "justifies" doing more today to control climate change. A high discount rate is dismissive of the future, and "justifies" doing much less on behalf of our descendants.

Return to the example of leaving $100 for your grandchildren 60 years from now, and consider the effects of the interest rate. At 1 percent interest, you have to put $55 in the bank today; at 3 percent, as mentioned above, $17 is enough; and at 5 percent, you need to deposit only $5 and change. The reason is that over a period of time as long as 60 years, compound interest is a powerful force. A higher interest rate lowers the amount you have to put in the bank today to reach the future target of $100; more of the work of getting to $100 is done for you by the accumulation of interest. A lower interest rate raises the amount you have to deposit, since less of the work of getting to $100 is done by the interest rate.

In the arena of climate economics, the same kind of calculations apply to the problem of valuing harmful future events, and to decisions about spending money now on prevention. The present value of $100 of damages 60 years from now is $55 at 1 percent, or $17 at 3 percent, or about $5 at 5 percent. In cost–benefit calculations, that present value is the maximum amount that is said to be economically rational to spend today to prevent the future harm. Spending more than that to prevent future damages would be "irrational" because it would in theory be cheaper to put the present value in a savings account, to compensate future generations for the damages when they occur.

If your grandchildren are threatened with a climate-related loss of $100 that will occur 60 years from now, is it economically rational to spend $55, or $17, or just $5 today to prevent that loss? This is why the choice of the discount rate is so important. For the same amount of threatened harm 60 years from now, the same type of economic analysis would endorse spending more than ten times as much on prevention today if the discount rate is 1 percent rather than 5 percent.

For longer time periods, the difference between high and low discount rates becomes even more drastic. Suppose that $1,000 of climate damages will occur 200 years from now. What is its present value, and therefore the maximum amount that should be spent (according to cost–benefit analysis) to prevent that damage? At a discount rate of 1 percent, the answer is $137; at 3 percent, it falls to less than $3; at 5 percent, it is less than $0.06. That is, seen through the lens of present value, costs and benefits that will occur 200 years from now are still visible, albeit diminished, at a 1 percent discount rate; they are tiny at 3 percent; and they are effectively invisible, reduced to mere pennies per thousand dollars, at 5 percent.

The examples so far have focused on a single cost or benefit, in a specific future year. In general, however, we are interested in comparing streams of costs and benefits that flow across many years. Consider the following example, still greatly simplified, but one step closer to the use of discounting in climate models. A proposed policy will cost $100 billion annually for the next hundred years. Spending that money will reduce climate damages, avoiding some of the harms that would be expected from business-as-usual emissions trends. That is, the benefits of the policy are the damages that it will avoid. Assume that those benefits start out at zero, but rise, faster and faster over time, reaching $600 billion annually by 100 years from now. These costs and benefits are shown in

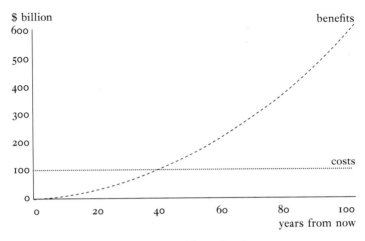

Figure 2.1   Costs and benefits, by year

Figure 2.1. (As in this illustration, the benefits of climate policy typically start out small but grow faster and faster over time, while costs begin immediately but do not rise as rapidly, if at all. The numbers used here were chosen for illustrative purposes; they are not actual data.[3])

Costs exceed benefits for the first 40 years, but benefits rise rapidly thereafter. By the time of your grandchildren, 60 years from now, the annual benefits are more than twice the annual costs. And the gap only widens in the following generation. Should this policy be adopted? Do its cumulative benefits exceed its cumulative costs?

The balance between costs and benefits depends entirely on the discount rate. As shown in Figure 2.2, the policy is a bargain at a 1 percent discount rate; the present value of the full century of

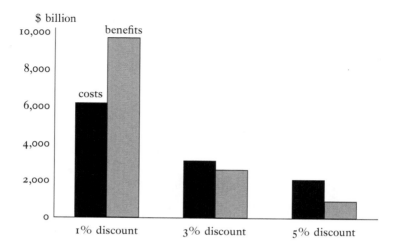

Figure 2.2   Present value of costs and benefits

benefits is about 50 percent greater than the present value of the corresponding costs. At a 3 percent discount rate, the balance has tipped in the opposite direction; the present value of benefits is just a little less than the costs. At 5 percent, the policy looks terrible, with benefits worth only about half of costs. In this example, the benefits of the policy exceed the costs at any discount rate below 2.45 percent; costs outweigh benefits at any rate above that.

The central role of the discount rate has been obvious from the beginnings of climate economics. There is a long-standing theoretical debate about how to choose the discount rate.[4] As the numerical examples suggest, the positions taken in this debate determine how expensive climate damages appear to be, and how much climate protection appears to be cost-effective.

Discount rates and financial markets

There are two broad families of theories about the discount rate, sometimes called "descriptive" and "prescriptive" approaches. The descriptive approach assumes that the discount rate should be equal to the market interest rate, or the rate of return on financial investments. Climate policy involves a number of investment decisions; the descriptive theory suggests that climate investments should be made on the same basis, with the same test for profitability, as any other investments. Thus the discount rate can simply be observed, by examining current or recent average rates of return in financial markets. It is common to conclude that investors in the stock market, for instance, can achieve long-term average rates of return of 5–7 percent. When numbers that large are used as the discount rate, as has been done in some well-known economic analyses, the game is over before it starts: at such high discount rates, the present value of the far future is insignificant, and very little climate protection can be justified by the present value of its benefits.

An alternative version of the descriptive approach reaches a very different conclusion.[5] To receive rates of return averaging as high as 5–7 percent above inflation, you have to make somewhat risky investments, like buying stocks. The rate of return on risk-free investments, such as government bonds, is much lower, averaging 1 percent or less above the rate of inflation. Which of these two rates should be used as the discount rate for climate policy? For investments with an average pattern of market risks, which go up and down along with the stock market, the rate of return based on the stock market would be appropriate. Investments in climate protection, however, bear a closer resemblance to insurance (more on that in the next chapter). Like insurance, climate protection is more useful when things turn out badly, and less valuable when all is going well. In other words, it is a risk-reducing investment; so the risk-free rate of return of 1 percent or less, some argue, is the appropriate discount rate for climate policy. At that discount rate, quite a lot of climate protection is justified by the present value of its future benefits.

The descriptive approach, in either variant, rests on an abstract theoretical hypothesis. In a textbook world of perfect markets and perfect rationality, in which everyone is well-informed and has access to financial markets, and everyone thinks about short-term private investments and long-term public policies in the same manner, the discount rate would be equal to the market rate of return. Both rates would express individuals' preferred trade-off between current and future incomes.

Reality, however, does not closely match that textbook world. In particular, there is no need for long-term policy decisions to be based on the same motives and calculations as short-term investments. One person could be narrowly focused on maximizing her own income from short-term decisions, and also expansively generous in making bequests to her grandchildren's generation. Someone else could be generous to the people around him today, but cynical about the future and uninterested in making bequests. There is no market in which short-term investments and long-term policies are traded against each other, so they need not follow the same logic or employ the same discount rate.

Discount rates and first principles

The other major theory of the discount rate, the prescriptive approach, builds up the discount rate from first principles. Using a framework that originated with an early twentieth-century econo-mist, Frank Ramsey,[6] it has become common to identify two separate motives for discounting, each contributing to the discount rate.

One component of the discount rate is based on the expected upward trend in income and wealth. If future generations will be much richer than we are, they will need less help from us, and they will get less benefit from an additional dollar of income than we do. So we can discount benefits that will flow to our wealthy descendants, at a rate based on the expected growth of per capita incomes. Conversely, if future generations turned out to be poorer than we are, as a result of climate catastrophes or other losses, they would need more help from us and would value an additional dollar more highly than we do. This would suggest that the discount rate should be less than zero, and $100 received in the future would have a present value of more than $100 today. Economic models and theories, however, almost always assume that incomes will grow, so that the income-related part of the discount rate will be greater than zero. Among economists, the income-related motive for discounting may be the least controversial part of the picture.

The other component of the discount rate is the rate that would apply if all generations had the same per capita income. It is called the rate of "pure time preference." There is a long-standing debate about whether or not the rate of pure time preference is zero; the debate involves ethical and philosophical arguments as well as economic theories.

On the one hand, there are reasons to think that pure time preference is greater than zero: both psychological experiments and common sense suggest that people are impatient, and prefer money now to money later. Thus people routinely act as if their pure time preference is positive. The strangest motivation for a positive rate of pure time preference (used in the Stern Review; see Chapter 7) is the observation that the human race may not survive for ever. If we were sure that the world was going to end next year, we undoubtedly would have one last party rather than saving for the future; in effect, our discount rate on future events would be enormous. So, if there is a tiny probability that life as we know it will not survive the coming year, due to a natural disaster or to one we inflict on ourselves (Stern's guess at the probability was 0.1 percent), there should be a corresponding, tiny contribution to the rate of pure time preference.

On the other hand, pure time preference of zero expresses the equal worth of people of all generations, and the equal importance of reducing climate impacts and other burdens on them (assuming that all generations have equal incomes). The question, according to climate scientist Stephen Schneider, is whether your granddaughter is less important than your daughter, simply because she will be born a generation later. Once again, private decisions within a single lifetime are different from public decisions spanning generations and centuries. It is possible to be impatient about the details of your own life, and at the same time to take a long view, based on the ethical issues of intergenerational equality, when it comes to your grandchildren and those who will follow them.

One more wrinkle in the economic theory of discounting should be mentioned. Although the discount rate has traditionally been treated as a constant over time, this is only an arbitrary simplifying assumption. Several creative theories have been developed explaining why discount rates should be expected to decline over time. This seems at first glance like a solution to some of the quandaries of discounting: the rate could start out high, then decline in the future. Unfortunately, this innovation has only a limited impact in practice. A high discount rate for the first few decades accomplishes most of the shrinkage of future values; after that, it does not much matter whether the rate goes down. In the examples above, a discount rate of 5 percent, applied for 60 years, reduced the present value of $100 to $5. Even if the discount rate then falls to a much lower level after 60 years, those initial six decades of high discounting still eliminate 95 percent of the value of all events that will occur farther into the future. It is, above all, the discount rate applied to the first few decades of the future that matters for climate economics.

The discount rate is the most important single number in climate economics, but it is not the only thing that matters. In order to clarify the role of discounting, the examples in this chapter have unrealistically assumed that all future costs and benefits are known in advance. Another fundamental question concerns uncertainty: how sure are we about those projected future costs and benefits that we are discounting? The answer – namely, that we are deeply and inescapably uncertain – turns out to have profound and surprising implications for economics, as explained in the next chapter.

3

We need to buy insurance for the planet

Climate change, studied by thousands of scientists around the world, is one of the best-researched issues in public life. Most policy decisions on other subjects, even the biggest ones, have to be made with much less information than we now have about our climate. Yet, paradoxically, we know that we don't know exactly what will happen next as the earth warms and the climate changes. This chapter explores the economic meaning of that uncertainty, explaining why it calls for greatly increased expenditures on climate protection. The goal, as we will see, is not only to respond to the predictable average changes, but, even more important, to prepare for the worst. Think of it as buying insurance for the planet.

The climate change card game

Does climate science tell us that we are uncertain about what will happen next? Or does it predict that things are certain to get worse? Unfortunately, the answer seems to be yes to both questions.

The problem is that different levels of uncertainty are involved. No one knows how to predict next year's weather, and the year-to-year variation is enormous: there could be many hurricanes next year, or almost none; unusually hot temperatures, or unusually mild; more rain, or less. But scientists now predict that we are headed toward both worsening average conditions and increasing variation around the average.

By way of analogy, imagine that you are drawing a card from a standard deck of fifty-two playing cards. You have no way to predict exactly what card you will draw, but you know a lot about the odds. There is exactly one chance in four of drawing a diamond, but any individual card may be a diamond, a club, a heart, or a spade. If you draw again and again, returning your card to the deck after each draw, then the average number on the cards you draw will be 7 (counting aces as 1, and jacks, queens, and kings as 11, 12, and 13) – but any individual draw could be much higher or lower than the average. This is what the weather might be like in the absence of climate change: plenty of fluctuation from one year to the next, but with familiar, unchanging averages and patterns of variation.

Now imagine that the dealer changes a card in the deck after each draw. If the dealer gradually removes all of the 6, 7, and 8 cards, there is no change in the average of the numbers you draw, but your chance of getting a very high or very low number in any one draw will increase. If the dealer adds extra cards with high numbers (face cards), and removes cards with low numbers, the average of the numbers you draw will increase.

The weather in a changing climate is like drawing a card from a changing deck. There is no good way of predicting the next card you will draw, or the next year's weather. But the deck of climate possibilities is changing in disturbing directions, both toward more variable and extreme weather, and toward worsening averages. There is even some uncertainty about how fast the deck is changing for the worse – although there is, sadly, more than enough evidence to rule out any hope that average conditions will remain unchanged.

Worst-case scenarios

Uncertainty and variability pose a challenge for economic analysis. To evaluate a proposal for spending money on climate protection, we need an estimate of how much damage it is protecting us from. How bad would things get without climate protection? How great would the climate-related damages be under a business-as-usual scenario, in the absence of any new climate initiatives? In order to apply cost–benefit analysis, it is not enough to know that the value of damages is uncertain and varies widely from year to year; some method for developing a single, summary estimate is needed.

One simple approach would be to ignore the uncertainties and only include the costs of climate changes that are certain, or definitely expected, to occur. This approach, used in many early economic models, omits much of what we know about climate risks and lowers the estimates of potential damages. Some newer models adopt a more sophisticated response, taking an average across a range of possibilities. This includes more of the picture, and yields higher estimates of expected damages. It is an improvement, but it still does not offer a complete understanding of climate risks.

Faced with uncertain, potentially large risks, people do not normally act on the basis of average outcomes; instead, they typically focus on protection against worst case scenarios. When you go to the airport, do you leave just enough time for the average amount of traffic delays (so that you would catch your plane, on average, half of the time)? Or do you allow time for some estimate of worst-case traffic jams? Once you get there, of course, you will experience additional delays due to security, which is all about worst cases: your *average* fellow passenger is not a threat to anyone's safety.

In science, 95 percent confidence is often considered sufficient to establish a result, but this is only an arbitrary convention. Having 95 percent confidence that we will avoid a disaster is not nearly enough; in ordinary life, people worry a great deal about things that have much less than a 5 percent chance of happening. The average US soldier in Iraq has more than a 95 percent chance – indeed, more than a 99 percent chance – of coming back alive from a tour of duty; this does not make fighting in Iraq a safe occupation.* In many areas of life, our decision-making is heavily influenced by catastrophic events with less than a 1 percent probability of occurrence.

The annual number of residential fires in the US is about 0.4 percent of the number of housing units.[1] This means that a fire occurs, on average, about once every 250 years in each home, not even close to once per lifetime. By far the most likely number of fires you will experience next year, or even in your lifetime, is zero. Why don't these statistics inspire you to cancel your fire insurance? Unless you are extremely wealthy, the loss of your home in a fire would be a devastating financial blow; despite the low probability, you cannot afford to take any chances on it.

What are the chances of the ultimate loss? The probability that you will die next year is under 0.1 percent if you are in your

---

* There are, in addition, many serious but nonfatal physical and psychological damages caused by warfare; one could not claim 95 percent confidence that a soldier would come back from Iraq entirely unharmed.

twenties, under 0.2 percent in your thirties, under 0.4 percent in your forties.[2] It is not until age 61 that you have as much as a 1 percent chance of death within the coming year. Yet most families with dependent children buy life insurance.[3] Without it, the risk to the children of losing the parents' income would be too great – even though the parents are, on average, extraordinarily likely to survive.

The very existence of the insurance industry is evidence of the desire to avoid or control worst-case scenarios. It is impossible for an insurance company to pay out in claims as much as its customers pay in premiums; if it did, there would be no money left to pay the costs of running the company, or the profits received by its owners.[*] People who buy insurance are therefore guaranteed to get back less than they, on average, have paid; they (we) are paying extra for the security that insurance provides, if the worst should happen. This way of thinking does not apply to every decision we make: in casino games, people make bets based on averages and probabilities, and no one sells you insurance against losing the next round. But life is not a casino, and public policy should not be a gamble.

Climate policy as insurance

Climate change involves both "ordinary," predictable damages, and much bigger, low-probability risks for which we would undoubtedly buy insurance if it were available. On the one hand, some climate impacts have a high probability of happening if we continue on our

---

[*] Insurance companies also invest the money they have received from premiums; in good years, their investment income may allow them to pay out more in claims than they receive in premiums. This is possible only because they receive the premiums long before they pay the resulting claims. In present value terms (see Chapter 2), the premiums are worth more than the amount paid out on claims.

present course – an average warming of several degrees over the course of this century, changes in precipitation patterns (with, it seems, many dry areas getting drier and wet areas getting wetter), a moderate rise in sea levels, increasing variability and intensification of weather extremes, and a host of disturbing consequences of these changes. These are bad enough, but they are not the most ominous climate problems that we may face.

There are also uncertain, lower-probability risks of abrupt, ir-reversible catastrophes, such as the complete collapse and melting of a major ice sheet. Loss of the Greenland ice sheet would raise sea levels by 7 meters (23 feet), inundating most of the world's coastal cities as well as the surrounding low-lying areas, displacing many millions of people, and destroying a large part of economic activity and infrastructure around the world. Loss of the West Antarctic ice sheet, which is also endangered, would have a similar-sized effect. It would take many years of melting for sea levels to rise by the full 7 meters, but the process would be unstoppable once it passed a tipping point. No one knows what probability to assign to these dangers, or when we would reach the tipping point, but everyone knows that ice becomes more likely to melt as temperatures rise.

The Intergovernmental Panel on Climate Change (IPCC), ex-pressing the consensus of the world's scientists, declared in its 2007 report that the collapse of a major ice sheet was not expected to occur in this century; that is, the probability is less than 50 percent, in the opinion of the IPCC. This is not, however, the only critical question. What we need to know is not only what is most likely to happen, but how bad are the outcomes that are as likely as the risks that people buy insurance against? What is the worst climate danger that is as likely as a house fire or the death of a young parent? Arrange all the possible climate outcomes in a line from best to worst; what does the 99th percentile worst outcome look like? (A house fire and the death of a young parent are both beyond the 99th percentile worst outcomes, as we have seen.)

It is hard to be 99 percent sure that the Greenland ice sheet will survive if temperatures rise by a few more degrees. Reports from Greenland suggest that ice is already melting faster than expected, and noticeably faster than just a few years ago. The same logic that leads to buying fire insurance and life insurance should lead to buying planetary insurance: doing whatever is needed to keep temperatures low enough to save the Greenland ice sheet and prevent 7 meters of sea-level rise. One widely discussed target, keeping temperature increases under 2°C (3.6°F), is often said to be what is required; this target is the lowest that seems achievable with a prompt and vigorous international response.

Loss of the Greenland ice sheet or its West Antarctic cousin is not the only potential climate catastrophe that will become more likely as temperatures rise. There is also a danger that the run-off from rapid melting of Greenland and the Arctic ice cap could slow down or shut off the thermohaline circulation in the North Atlantic. Colloquially, this would turn off the Gulf Stream and would thereby make the North Atlantic much colder, an outcome that was presented in theatrically exaggerated form by the 2004 movie *The Day After Tomorrow*. (Theatrics aside, there is some evidence suggesting that this happened during the rapid warming after the end of the last ice age, resulting in a thousand or more years of extremely cold weather before the thermohaline circulation resumed.[4]) Another threat is that rising temperatures might at some point trigger an abrupt, massive release of methane, either from thawing tundra or from undersea rock formations; the additional global warming impact of all that methane could lead to a much accelerated, runaway greenhouse effect. And there are other risks: for example, forest and soil sequestration of carbon could fall sharply as temperatures rise past critical thresholds, releasing large amounts of carbon dioxide and methane.

None of these catastrophes is predicted to occur in the near future, and the more exotic catastrophes may be less likely than the loss of the Greenland ice sheet. The exact probabilities, and the tipping points at which they become unstoppable, are unknown. But, as with melting ice sheets, they become more likely as temperatures rise. Any of them would make much of the world uninhabitable, with devastating human, ecological, and economic losses. Climate protection offers a comprehensive insurance package, covering a wide range of dangers. Is the risk of possible catastrophes enough to inspire us to buy the insurance package?

Incalculable risks

An objection might be raised to the insurance analogy. Do we know, in fact, that the loss of the Greenland ice sheet or other potential catastrophes are as probable as the risks for which people buy insurance? Have they reached the level of a few tenths of a percent (i.e. a few chances per thousand) per year, or will they soon, as temperatures rise? If we had thousands of similar planets available, we could find out the probabilities of catastrophe by the experimental method. Unfortunately, having only one planet for our use, we have to get the answer right the first time, without waiting for empirical evidence.

According to Harvard economist Martin Weitzman, the probabilities of the worst outcomes are inescapably unknowable – and this deep uncertainty should be more important than anything we do know in motivating concern about climate change. The stories about fire insurance and life insurance involve qualitatively less uncertainty; they are cases of what could be called "known unknowns." You do not know whether or not you will have a fire next year or die before the year is over, but you have very good information about the likelihood of these tragic events. So does the insurance industry, which is why they are willing to insure you. The worst case is extremely bad for you, but it is well defined and has a known probability.

Even the card game story that opened this chapter, as an analogy to variable and changing climate conditions, contains an unwarranted bit of predictability. Although the dealer in that story was gradually changing the cards and thereby could change the average number that would be drawn, the only cards in use were the standard ones: the ace, 2 through 10, jack, queen, and king. If the number or face on the card represents how good or bad climate conditions will be, then using only the familiar cards corresponds to assuming that nothing outside the known, historical range of variation will occur. There were no jokers or wild cards, representing unexpectedly drastic outcomes, in the deck.

Climate change is causing average temperatures and other conditions to move outside the known, familiar range of variation. Both the European heatwave of 2003 and the US hurricane season of 2005 are unwelcome omens of a more dangerously variable climate in years to come. During this century, if present trends continue, the earth will reach average temperatures well outside the range for which there is any direct observational experience to draw on. What happens to massive ice sheets at those temperatures? The edges and the surface melt a bit faster, of course; but how fast does water seep through the cracks to the bottom? Once it is there, how much does it lubricate and accelerate the ice sliding toward the ocean? When does that process become unstoppable? These and other questions about the tipping points for climate catastrophes cannot be answered with certainty, either from theory or from experience.

A modified version of the card game analogy may capture this deeper uncertainty. This version of the game may sound more confusing, and is surrounded with so much uncertainty that you would never choose to bet on it – but that's the point. We are, metaphorically, playing a game much like this with climate uncertainty, and betting all our chips on its outcome.

Once again, suppose that you are repeatedly drawing a numbered card from a deck; the bigger the number, the worse the climate will be. The difference is, the cards are no longer restricted to just the familiar ones, and you do not know in advance how high the numbers on the cards can go. Assume the deck contains 100 cards, so that each card has a 1 percent probability of being drawn each time. As before, your card is shuffled back into the deck after each draw. Can you figure out, from the cards you draw, what is the highest number in the deck? In terms of the underlying analogy, the highest number represents the worst case, or 99th percentile bad outcome, for climate damages.

By drawing repeatedly from a 100-card deck that never changed, you could eventually learn everything about the deck. The process, however, would be slow: you would need to draw about 70 times to have a fifty-fifty chance of seeing the highest card, and about 300 times to have 95 percent confidence that you had seen it.[5]

Now assume that the dealer is changing one card after every draw. This means that old information is becoming outdated as fast as new information is arriving; in effect, you will never have more than a limited sample on which to base your judgments. You will never know with much confidence, therefore, what the worst card, representing the 99th percentile climate risk, looks like. Yet, as we have seen, 99th percentile dangers loom large in decision-making about catastrophic risks.

The moral of this story applies to more than climate change; indeed, it was first developed in an analysis of financial markets, another arena where people worry about unknown worst cases. In any system that is so complex that its behavior is not fully predictable (the highest card is unknown), and is changing so quickly that old data become irrelevant as fast as new data arrive (the dealer is changing the cards), it is impossible to estimate the probability of worst-case risks. If – as in the case of climate change – there is no limit to the costs that could result from those worst cases, then there is also no limit to how much should be spent on risk reduction.

How sensitive is the climate?

Weitzman, the economist who developed the mathematical analysis behind the card game analogy,* suggests that it could apply to the problem of estimating the so-called "climate sensitivity parameter." That parameter measures the severity of climate change; it is defined as the long-term temperature increase that will eventually result from a doubling of carbon dioxide concentrations in the atmosphere. If current emission trends continue, the world will reach CO_2 concentrations of double the pre-industrial level within a few decades. The climate sensitivity parameter is one numerical measure of how bad that heightened CO_2 level will turn out to be.

* He is not to blame for the card game, which is my attempt at a simple analogy to his staggeringly complex mathematical results.

To apply the card game analogy, each card can now be thought of as a piece of experimental evidence that provides an empirical estimate of the climate sensitivity parameter.

There is enough evidence to rule out zero as an option for the climate sensitivity parameter – which is another way of saying that climate change really is happening. There is not enough information, however, to determine the precise value of the parameter – that is, the ultimate severity of climate change – with any certainty. The IPCC's best guess, as of 2007, was that the climate sensitivity parameter was 3°C, with a likely range from 2°C to 4.5°C (or 5.4°F, with a likely range from 3.6°F to 8.1°F). Weitzman constructs a plausible argument that, based on our current knowledge, the 99th percentile value of the climate sensitivity parameter could be 10°C (18°F) – and he claims that additional harmful effects of warming, not included in the climate sensitivity estimates, could double that warming, for an eventual 20°C (36°F). With or without the final doubling, this is a truly catastrophic temperature increase. As Weitzman puts it,

> such high temperatures have not been seen for hundreds of millions of years... Because such hypothetical temperature changes would be geologically instantaneous, it would effectively destroy planet Earth as we know it. At a minimum this would trigger mass species extinctions and biosphere ecosystem disintegration matching or exceeding the immense planetary die-offs associated with a handful of such previous geoclimate mega-catastrophes in Earth's history.[6]

Recall that this is a description of the 99th percentile risk of climate impacts, from CO_2 levels that could be reached through just a few more decades of business as usual. No one has suggested that it is certain, or even the most likely outcome, of climate change. Most

99th percentile risks don't ever occur, just as most houses never have fires and most parents live to see their children grow up.

And yet we buy insurance when faced with individual risks of this likelihood or even less. We don't generally complain to our insurance company about its high premiums when we turn out, like almost everyone, to avoid fires and stay alive. Instead, we sleep better at night, knowing that we are insured against the worst that could happen. Shouldn't we buy fire insurance for everybody's house, and life insurance for the human race, by immediately reducing global emissions? Suppose that we, or more likely our descendants, were to discover someday that we had paid for a bit more wind and solar power than was absolutely needed, in hindsight, to prevent a climate catastrophe. How badly would history remember us for that mistake?

4

Climate damages are too valuable to have prices

In order to make good decisions about climate policy, do we need more information about the value of the expected damages from global warming, or about the costs of preventing them? The last two chapters presented two strong reasons to conclude that the answer is no. The discount rate, the subject of Chapter 2, dominates any long-term cost–benefit calculation: many climate policies appear to be cost-effective at a low discount rate, while almost none are at a high discount rate. The discount rate is a matter of political and ethical judgment about our responsibility to future generations, not a problem amenable to scientific or economic research. As a result, the question of how much to do about climate change is a non-technical, political decision – even if cloaked in the form of a debate about discount rates and economic theory.

The uncertainty about low-probability, catastrophic risks, the subject of Chapter 3, upstages any ordinary calculations of costs and benefits. In many areas of life, people worry about, and buy insurance against, disastrous outcomes – such as residential fires, or deaths of young and middle-aged adults – that have annual probabilities measured in tenths of a percent. One can infer from the latest IPCC reports that there is at least a 1 percent chance that disastrously increased warming will render much of the world uninhabitable. Thus it is time to buy insurance against worst-case outcomes for the planet, not to fine-tune the estimates of what is most likely to happen.

And yet almost everyone remains fascinated with "bottom line" estimates of costs and benefits. Elizabeth Stanton and I produced an extensively researched, hundred-page account of numerous expected impacts of climate change in Florida, many of which are vividly detailed but could not be priced.[1] Virtually every article or commentary mentioning that report focused exclusively on our calculation for the four categories of damages where we did estimate dollar values.

There is a puzzle lurking here about the sociology of numbers: is the single-minded focus on dollar estimates a sign that people are more comfortable conversing about money and numbers, as opposed to complex verbal descriptions? Or does it show that people are *un*comfortable with numbers, and hence easily impressed by them? My suspicion is that the latter is at least part of the story. But whatever its basis, the ongoing fascination with dollar estimates means that the costs and benefits of climate change will continue to be studied and debated for the foreseeable future. This chapter addresses the problems of valuing the benefits of climate policy; the next chapter turns to the costs.

Monetary values for the benefits of climate policy tend to understate the urgency of the problem, in two different ways: some of the most important benefits have no meaningful prices; and some economic models minimize the benefits by suggesting that a little bit of global warming would be good for us.

Expensive, or priceless?

The benefits of climate policy are the damages that can be avoided by taking action to reduce emissions (or sequester carbon, or successfully adapt to the unavoidable changes), rather than allowing present trends to continue. The calculation of benefits often involves developing best guesses about two future scenarios: a business-as-usual scenario based on extrapolating present emissions and climate trends, with no new policies; and a policy scenario estimating how the future will evolve if a proposed new policy is adopted. The difference between the greater damages under business-as-usual and the lesser damages under the policy scenario is the benefit of adopting the policy. Or, equivalently, the difference between the scenarios can be seen as the cost of inaction.

Climate damages are measured in many different units, including numbers of deaths, losses of acres of wetlands and other ecosystems, and losses of income, among others. If they all came with price tags attached, the dollar value of the benefits of climate policy could be found by subtracting one scenario's total damages from the other. However, the impacts of climate change are a mixture of things that are expensive and things that are priceless. The priceless impacts are often the most important, yet they are difficult or impossible to represent in monetary terms.[2]

In our study of Florida, we found that the state will be hard hit if current trends in emissions and warming continue over the course of this century, even without any of the abrupt, catastrophic effects discussed in Chapter 3. Hurricanes will become more intense and damaging, harming more property and killing more people. Much of south Florida will be at risk of inundation from sea-level rise within this century, including large parts of the Miami metropolitan area as well as the unique ecosystems and endangered species of the Everglades, the Keys, and other low-lying areas. (This is the projected result of just a few feet of sea-level rise, the amount expected over the course of this century; vastly greater areas of the state would be at risk if a major ice sheet were to melt, causing a few *dozen* feet of sea-level rise). Tourism, the state's largest industry, will suffer as damage to beaches and other coastal areas, combined with hotter, stormier weather, will reduce the attractiveness of outdoor recreation. Changes in rainfall patterns will worsen the state's ongoing water crisis, which is already prompting an expensive search for nontraditional water supplies.

What could it mean to produce a single dollar figure for all of these damages? Among the most important impacts of unchecked climate change are the increased losses of human lives. If these are excluded from monetary calculations on the grounds that they have no price, any dollar estimate of climate damages is crucially incomplete. If, on the other hand, they are to be included, we need to know the price of a human life. Think for a minute, before reading on, about how you would invent this non-existent number. If it was up to you, how would the price of a human life be determined?

Would you propose that a price could be assigned to human lives by studying the difference in wages between slightly more and less dangerous jobs, and assuming that the difference represents the "price" of the increased risk of death?[3] That approach was adopted by EPA analysts in the 1990s. Suppose that workers who face an annual risk of death on the job of 1 in 10,000 (a typical risk for male blue-collar workers in the US) receive about $0.30 per hour, or $600 per year, more than comparable workers with no risk of death on the job. On this basis, 1/10,000th of a life would be worth $600; a whole life would be worth 10,000 times as much, or $6 million – which is roughly the EPA estimate from the late 1990s.

Or would you feel that it was more scientific to ask a few people how much they would spend for a small reduction in the risk of death? This approach was favored by the second Bush administration, starting in 2001. For this method of valuation, people are asked to fill out long questionnaires, asking what they would pay for a small change in risk under abstract, hypothetical scenarios. The willingness to pay for a small risk reduction can then be scaled up, just as with the wage risk calculations. If a survey found that people would be willing to pay $3.70 to avoid a one in a million risk of death, then the estimated value of a life would be $3.7 million, a figure often used by Bush administration analysts. As these examples suggest, the survey method resulted in lower values per life than the wage risk method, and thus fewer environmental policies were able to pass a cost–benefit test under the Bush administration – but that was not the (stated) purpose of the shift to survey-based values.

Neither of these methods comes close to capturing the profound meaning of a preventable human death, or a life saved. Ethical judgments about life and death are not measured by small wage differentials for risky jobs, or by surveys asking a small sample of the population to answer hypothetical questions about minute risks. Nor is there any research agenda that can lead to a more meaningful dollar value of a life; the problem is that it is an unreasonable question to be asking in the first place.

There is no good answer, but there are plenty of bad ones. In one chapter of the IPCC's 1995 report, a group of economists proposed that the value of a life should be fifteen times as high in rich countries as in the poorest parts of the world. If you believe that the value of a life depends on willingness to pay for risk reduction, which has some connection with ability to pay, or income, then this is a logical, understandable result. If, on the other hand, you believe in the equal worth of all human beings, the income-based value of a life is absurd and offensive. The latter turns out to be a popular view: widespread outrage over the unequal valuations of life erupted a little too late to change the 1995 report, but led to explicit condemnation of such approaches in the next IPCC report in 2001.[4]

Another dimension of inequality is introduced by the more recent proposal to assign a value to each year of life rather than each life. The result would be that younger lives are "worth" much more than older ones. There is a superficial appeal to this proposal: isn't it more important to save a child with a life expectancy of seventy years, rather than a senior citizen who might well die of something else in just a few more years? Yet the proposal *should* be controversial. Which of the world's major religions, ethical beliefs, and legal systems maintain that it is a lesser crime to kill an older person?

The age bias of life-year calculations is of particular importance for air pollution and climate change: fossil fuel combustion, the source of most carbon dioxide emissions, also produces other air pollutants that cause serious respiratory and other diseases. Those diseases cause thousands of deaths, especially among the elderly. How much should we spend to reduce air pollution and prevent some of those deaths? Cost–benefit analysis, using valuation based on life-years, could produce a disturbing answer: "Not much, since they were going to die soon anyway."

Any price for lives, high or low, creates the misleading impression that they can be traded for other things of comparable value. Investing $100 now in a project that pays $300 ten years from is a financial success: it is equivalent to an annual rate of return of more than 11 percent, and the later gains more than compensate the investor for the initial cost. A policy that kills 100 people now in order to save 300 other lives ten years from now is not equally successful: there is no way to compensate the 100 people who paid the initial cost.

A bargain at twice the price

Other priceless damages caused by climate change include the destruction of ecosystems and the potential extinction of endangered species. One straightforward, though limited, measure of value rests on the price of the services provided by ecosystems: for instance, clean rivers supply us with clean water, saving the expense of water purification that is needed when rivers are polluted. Ecosystem services provide an important but incomplete valuation of nature; many unique locations and endangered species have a value to people far beyond any measurable services that they supply.

To address the value of nature more comprehensively, economists have asked people how much nature is worth to them. (In addition to its other flaws, this method necessarily omits any value of nature beyond its value to humans.) There do not appear to be any valuation studies for the species most immediately threatened by climate change, such as polar bears or coral reefs, but the same questions have been asked about other species. What, for example, is it worth to protect whales from extinction? Some years ago, a survey estimated that the US population would pay $18 billion to protect the existence of humpback whales.[5] The corresponding global willingness to pay would of course be several times larger. But a moment's thought shows that any such number contains no real information.

Imagine a multibillionaire who offers to pay twice the stated value – $36 billion for the US alone, proportionally more for the world as a whole – for the right to hunt and kill all the humpback whales in the ocean. It is clear that the offer itself is offensive, and the price doesn't matter. This is quite unlike an offer to buy your car for twice its value: whether or not you accept such an offer, you are unlikely to be offended by it; and the price does matter. Rather, the offer to "buy" a species for exclusive private use is categorically unacceptable, just as an offer to buy your spouse or children would be. Your car is a commodity with a meaningful monetary price. Your family, your life (or anyone else's), and the existence of whales and other species, are not commodities; it is offensive and misleading to treat them as if they were for sale at any price.

The discussion of values without prices has a long history. As the eighteenth-century philosopher Immanuel Kant put it, some things have a price, or relative worth, while other things have a dignity, or inner worth.[6] No price tag does justice to the dignity of human life or the natural world. Since some of the most important benefits of climate protection are priceless, any monetary value for total benefits will necessarily be incomplete.

A craving for heat

Several economists writing about climate change have focused on a very different issue of incompleteness: they have included estimates of the benefits of moderate warming, offsetting some of the damages it will cause. Does climate change have a good side, as well as a bad? Will a little bit of global warming make us happier, healthier, or richer? At least three potential reasons to embrace the early stages of warming have appeared in leading economic models: the subjective enjoyment of warmth; projected reductions in mortality; and gains to northern agriculture. All three appear to be partially or entirely misleading.

The supposed benefits of warming loom large in the work of William Nordhaus.[7] Based largely on the fact that Americans spend more on summer than on winter outdoor recreation, Nordhaus has concluded that there is a huge subjective desire, and willingness to pay, for hotter weather in cold northern countries. In his view, people worldwide feel that the optimal temperature is a year-round average of 20°C (68°F). This is well above the current global average; it is the temperature of Houston or New Orleans in the United States, or Tripoli in Libya.

There are many people who live in areas of the world that are hotter than Houston, but they are generally poorer than the people who live in areas colder than Houston. If willingness to pay is limited by ability to pay (i.e. tied to income), there is a large net global willingness to pay for warming, at least until places like Chicago, New York, and London start to feel at hot as Houston. In the previous (2000) version of Nordhaus's model, this factor outweighed all climate damages worldwide and implied net benefits from warming until the middle of this century. The 2007 version of the same model retreats, but only slightly, from the earlier claim: it still assumes the same craving for heat, but no longer projects net global benefits from warming.

In reality, subjective attitudes toward temperatures might well depend on how the question is framed. Should people be asked whether they would enjoy a slightly warmer temperature, all else being equal? Or is the question whether they would enjoy a slightly warmer temperature in the short run, if it meant taking another step along the road to more extreme and damaging climate change in the long run? Residents of cold northern areas might well answer yes to the first question – but the second one is the only one that matters. Even as an answer to the first question, the Nordhaus estimate may overstate the subjective value of warming. Survey research examining actual attitudes toward climate conditions has produced far smaller estimates of the psychological benefits of warmer temperatures, suggesting that only a few of the northernmost countries will enjoy even the first decades of climate change.[8]

Is hotter weather healthier?

Another potential benefit which some economists anticipate from the early stages of warming is a large reduction in temperature-related deaths. Bjørn Lomborg, a leading anti-environmentalist, highlights the mortality reduction from warming in his latest attack on climate policy (see Chapter 6). Lomborg draws heavily on an academic study that makes the remarkable prediction that about 2°F of global warming will, on balance, save more than 800,000 lives annually by 2050.[9] This prediction starts with a surprising fact, and then proceeds to exaggerate its importance wildly. The surprising fact is that short-term temperature changes affect death rates, especially for people over 65 suffering from cardiovascular and respiratory diseases. Deaths increase on both cold and hot days, but more temperature-related deaths occur when it is colder than the local ideal temperature – which is typically a little below the local summer average temperature. Note the importance of *local* temperatures:

according to another study, the ideal, mortality-minimizing temperature is 9°C (15°F) higher in Miami than in Chicago.[10]

As Chicago and other cold places heat up due to global warming, will the local ideal temperature be unchanged? If so, then there would be fewer days that are colder than the ideal, and hence fewer deaths. It seems much more likely, however, that the local ideal temperature will gradually increase, along with the warming trend in the climate. People do move from cold northern cities to Miami and other warm places, and adapt relatively quickly to the new temperatures they experience. If people adapt to the gradually rising average temperature as the world warms, then there will be just as many "cold" days as before, relative to the changing definition of "cold" – and no reason to forecast a reduction in cold-related deaths. (In addition, there are a number of other technical errors that lead to exaggeration in the forecast of more than 800,000 lives per year saved by warming.[11])

Yet another study, using detailed, county-level data on US death rates and temperatures, projected that warming will cause a small (statistically insignificant) *increase* in deaths. That study suggests that this century's increase in hot days will come largely at the expense of fewer mild, moderate-temperature days; there will be more hot days per year than at present, but almost the same number of cold days. It is the mild, pleasant days when death rates are lowest; so fewer moderate-temperature days would result in a higher death rate for the year.[12]

Agriculture in a warmer world

A more believable, but nonetheless probably mistaken, prediction of gains from warming involves the impacts on agriculture. Early studies of climate impacts suggested substantial agricultural gains from warming, as a result of longer growing seasons in high latitudes and the effects of CO_2 fertilization on many crops.[13] Plants grow by absorbing CO_2 from the atmosphere and using the carbon; more CO_2 could therefore act as a fertilizer, speeding up growth. A handful of plants, including corn, sorghum, and sugar cane, already absorb CO_2 so efficiently that this fertilization effect won't help them; most other plants could in theory grow faster if they took in a little more carbon from the air.

Successive studies, however, have reduced the estimated importance of CO_2 fertilization. Outdoor experiments have shown smaller effects of CO_2 fertilization than earlier experiments conducted in greenhouses.[14] Moreover, some researchers project that the negative effects of ground-level ozone, which is produced by the same fossil fuel combustion processes that emit CO_2, may offset the impacts of a longer growing season and CO_2 fertilization and lead to a net decrease in agricultural productivity in the US.[15]

Another study approaches the question by an indirect route, and suggests that warming might not increase US farm output.[16] It assumes that the market value of farmland is a good indicator of its agricultural productivity; after all, what else could explain the price of an acre of farmland? In areas of the US where there is little or no irrigation, the market value of farmland is highly correlated with the climate. The maximum value per acre occurs at roughly the current average temperature, and somewhat more than the current average rainfall. This implies that US farmland would be more productive, on average, if it became wetter – but not if it became warmer. Using this relationship, the study projects that climate change through the end of the century will result in substantial losses in farm value. The losses reflect crop damage from the projected increase in the number of days above 34°C (93°F), a temperature that is bad for virtually all crops. The same researchers did a similar study of California, where most farms are irrigated; there the value of farmland is closely linked to the amount of irrigation water that is applied to the land, but not to temperature or precipitation.[17]

Most of this discussion has focused on the United States; from a global perspective, the outlook for agriculture in a warming world is even worse. In hotter and more tropical areas, there is even less reason to suspect that climate change could be good for farming; instead, there will be more days that are too hot for virtually all crops. North America is colder than Africa, the Middle East, South Asia, and much of Latin America – and it is the hotter regions that will suffer more immediately from climate change. So if climate change looks bad for US farmers, it will be even worse for their counterparts around the world. Whether or not the US experiences increased crop yields, it (along with Canada, Russia, and other colder areas) will produce an increased percentage of world food output, as yields decline elsewhere.

There will undoubtedly be some economic benefits from warming, especially in northern areas. People will pay less and use less energy for heating; snow removal costs and other directly winter-related expenditures will be reduced. But these are small in the overall picture, and will be outweighed by increased expenditures and energy use for air conditioning in areas that become uncomfortably hot. There is no reason to think that the good side to global warming is large enough to affect the balance of costs and benefits, just as there is no reason to think that any dollar figure fully represents the value of climate damages, or the benefits of climate protection.

In the end, we know that the damages of unchecked climate change, of accepting business as usual, will be large and growing. There is no hope of coming up with a single dollar amount that adequately summarizes the full range of climate impacts; too many of the impacts are incapable of being measured in monetary terms. Yet even without an impossibly comprehensive summary number, there are ample grounds for taking action to reduce climate damages.

5

Some costs are better than others

What will it cost to do something about climate change? While this is not an easy question to answer, it is less difficult than pricing the benefits. As discussed in the last chapter, the benefits of climate protection involve the priceless values of human life, nature, and the future. In contrast, the costs largely consist of producing and buying goods and services – in other words, things that have prices.

It is routinely easier to put prices on the costs of regulation than on the benefits. For short-term environmental problems with well-defined technical solutions, it may even be possible to create objective, transparent cost estimates based on "hard data" that are accepted by all. The 2000–2001 debate over the US standard for arsenic in drinking water is a good example: while there was intense technical and partisan conflict over EPA's estimates and valuation of the health benefits of reduced exposure to arsenic, no one challenged EPA's detailed engineering cost estimates for numerous options for removing arsenic from water systems.[1]

Unfortunately, there is little hope of transparent, uncontroversial estimates for the costs of climate policy. Although there are plenty of engineering estimates for specific technologies, a complete picture of the costs of climate protection inextricably involves economic theories as well as empirical data. A conventional economic framework, of the sort described in Chapter 1, tends to overstate the cost of climate protection on several timescales:

- in the short run, theories of market equilibrium often deny the existence of costless or negative-cost opportunities for emissions reduction;
- in the medium term, the same theories overlook the employment and other benefits that result from climate policies;
- in the long term, the most important effect is the pace of innovation in energy technologies, another subject on which conventional economics has little to offer.

Energy savings without costs

There are two rival approaches to calculating the costs of saving energy and reducing emissions. The bottom-up approach begins with detailed information on individual technologies and options, adding them up to create an estimate of total costs. The top-down approach looks at the economy, or major parts of it, as a whole, analyzing the likely response to price changes and other influences. The most important difference between the two approaches is that bottom-up studies routinely estimate that significant energy conservation can be done for no net cost – that is, households and businesses have not made all of the cost-effective expenditures on energy conservation that are currently available. The top-down approach, relying on economic theory, often assumes that costless energy savings are impossible.

Costless opportunities for energy savings can be found in many sectors, but are particularly common in buildings, appliances, and lighting choices. More and better building insulation, new energy-efficient lighting, and newer appliances would often save money on energy bills at today's prices. The effect will be even stronger, making it worthwhile to invest in more insulation and more efficient use of electricity, if a tax on carbon emissions is introduced or if energy prices continue to rise.

According to the IPCC's 2007 report, costless savings – "no regrets" options, in the jargon of climate negotiation – could reduce annual emissions by 6 gigatons (billion tons) of CO_2 equivalent, or 10 percent of global emissions, by 2030.[2] That potential does not depend on any new policy, tax or other price on carbon emissions; it is simply based on opportunities to save money at current market prices. With a carbon tax – or higher market prices for fossil fuels, which would have the same effect – even greater savings would become cost-effective. IPCC estimated that it would be cost-effective to eliminate 15 to 30 percent of greenhouse gas emissions at a carbon tax of $20 per ton of CO_2; that is roughly equivalent to a tax increase of $0.20 per gallon of gasoline, or a price increase of $10 per barrel of oil along with proportional increases in coal and gas prices. Elimination of as much as 30 to 50 percent of emissions would be cost-effective at a carbon tax of $100 per ton of CO_2, roughly equivalent to a $1.00 tax per gallon of gasoline or an oil price hike of almost $50 per barrel.

Recent studies from McKinsey & Company, an international consulting firm, reached conclusions similar to the IPCC.[3] Their global estimate was that by 2030, as much as 6 gigatons of CO_2

equivalent emissions per year could be eliminated at negative or zero net cost, and 26 gigatons at a cost of €40 (about $60, as of early 2008) per ton of CO_2. In a subsequent study of US emissions and reduction opportunities, McKinsey estimated that 1.4 gigatons of emissions could be eliminated at no net cost, a figure that rises to 3 gigatons, or almost one-third of US emissions in 2030, at a cost of $50 per ton of CO_2 equivalent. Oil prices may already have climbed high enough to make this larger reduction cost-effective.[4]

Costless energy savings are, according to a long-standing tradition in economic theory, impossible. In the textbook model of a competitive market economy, every resource is productively employed in its most valuable use, and every no-regrets option has already been taken. The standard metaphors for this concept are well known: there is no such thing as a free lunch; there are no $20 bills on the sidewalk, because someone would have picked them up already. Top-down models of climate costs, based on economic theory, do not include free lunches. In these models, all emissions reductions have positive costs, starting low for the first rounds of reduction and rising as the targets become more ambitious. This leads to a picture of climate policy costs quite different from the bottom-up models with their extensive opportunities for costless savings.

Although it is repeatedly contradicted by empirical evidence, the no-free-lunch theory does not sound silly in the abstract. After all, in a literal, non-metaphorical sense, $20 bills do not spend much time on the sidewalk. Why should big savings be persistently available for free throughout the field of energy use? Some of the projected savings could have hidden costs associated with them, so that they are not actually free. However, there are several reasons why truly costless savings could be lying on the sidewalk, waiting to be picked up.[5]

The obstacle may be as simple as a lack of information: in a world of rapid changes in both energy technologies and prices, many people are understandably unfamiliar with the latest cost-effective opportunities. The remedy for this problem, public education about what's available and why it saves money, has to be one of the cheapest possible ways to reduce emissions.

Another obstacle could be lack of access to financing: many of the costless opportunities require an up-front investment, which will pay for itself through reduced energy bills. An energy-saving investment of $600 that reduces your energy bills by $25 per month has a two-year payback period; twenty-four months of savings repay the investment, and everything you save after that is pure profit. This makes it an incredibly good deal compared to most things you could do with $600 – but you have to have the whole $600 available at the start, rather than spreading the cost out over your next twenty-four monthly bills. Financial guarantees for energy-saving investments could help overcome this obstacle, encouraging households and small businesses to make the numerous financially attractive investments in energy conservation that are available today.

A deeper structural obstacle is the fragmented nature of the housing market. Many decisions that affect the energy efficiency of a building are made by home builders, who often suspect that buyers will not be willing to pay for additional energy-saving features. Yet it is the buyers who will pay the energy costs, and would have benefited from a more energy-conscious design. In rental properties, there is a further fragmentation: landlords suspect that tenants will not pay higher rents for more energy-efficient homes; tenants, who usually pay the energy costs, will not make investments with multi-year payback periods, because they may not be there to enjoy the benefits. Thus the potential for improving the energy efficiency of buildings cannot be realized, because there are many cost-effective investments which no one has an incentive to make. Better information about the value of energy-efficient buildings would help overcome this obstacle, as would changes in building codes and appliance standards to require high levels of insulation, state-of-the-art efficiency in new appliances, and other energy-saving measures.

Good costs and bad costs

The no-regrets options for energy conservation and emissions reduction are the obvious first steps toward a sustainable, low-carbon future. The question of costs hardly arises in these early stages; there are only minimal public costs for the additional public education, financing guarantees, and changes in regulations and incentives that are needed to achieve this potential. The projected magnitude of the available costless savings is encouraging – but it is far below 100 percent of what is needed to maintain a tolerable climate for future generations. As we (hopefully) move rapidly through the costless savings, the basic question recurs: how much will it cost to finish the job?

The answer is, once again, that there are rival interpretations of the costs, based on rival assumptions and theories about the economy. One perspective views all costs as making people worse off; the alternative distinguishes between good costs and bad costs, seeking to have more of one and less of the other. Think of it as the cholesterol model of climate costs.

The same economic theory that proclaimed the absence of free lunches and $20 bills on the sidewalk is responsible for the idea that all costs are bad. Since the free market lets everyone spend their money in whatever way makes them happiest, any new cost forced on them from outside must represent a loss: it leaves everyone with less to spend on whatever purchases they had previously selected to maximize their satisfaction in life. Climate damages are one source of loss, and spending on climate protection is another; both reduce the resources available for the desirable things in life. This perspective is the motivation for cost–benefit analysis: you wouldn't want to spend more on climate protection than the value of the damages it avoids.

But are the two kinds of costs really comparable? Suppose that the choices were spending $1 billion on bigger and better levees, or not building the levees and losing $1 billion to storm damages. Money spent on building levees creates jobs and incomes. The construction workers will go home and buy groceries, clothing, and so on, indirectly creating other jobs. With more people working, tax revenues will increase while unemployment compensation payments will decrease.

None of this happens if the levees are not built, and the storm damages are allowed to occur. The costs of prevention are good costs, with numerous indirect benefits; the costs of climate damages are bad costs, representing pure physical destruction. One worthwhile goal is to keep all costs as low as possible; another is to have as much as possible of the costs related to climate change be good costs rather than bad costs.

If all storm damages were reversible, and there was an ironclad guarantee that all damages would be repaired, the same indirect economic benefits would accrue later, from the repair process. In fact, some damages, such as deaths, are irreversible, and it is hard to be sure that all necessary repairs will occur. The botched, incomplete recovery from Hurricane Katrina does not inspire confidence about the US response to future disasters. The destruction of large parts of New Orleans and other nearby communities by Hurricane Katrina is the epitome of bad costs, of physical loss without any redeeming indirect benefits. Adequate levees to protect New Orleans could have been built for a small fraction of the cost of the property damages that did occur in 2005 – to say nothing of the loss of lives and livelihoods that ensued.

The opposite picture, the iconic image of good costs, spending money to protect against storm surges and rising seas, can be seen in the Netherlands. Long famous for its dikes protecting low-lying areas, the Netherlands was spurred to take further protective action by an extraordinarily powerful and deadly storm in 1953. Since that time, decades of expensive investment have built better, higher, and more extensive protection from the sea. This may not be a perfect or permanent solution to the problems of rising seas and stormy weather, but it has successfully protected the country for many years. The Dutch economy depends on it; parts of Amsterdam's Schiphol airport, one of Europe's busiest, lie below sea level.[6]

No one appears to have been impoverished by this enormous protective investment. On the contrary, the Netherlands is one of the world's most affluent countries. Would the Dutch have been better off building less extensive sea walls and barriers, taking a greater chance on damages from extreme storms in order to have even more money for private consumption? It is easier to believe the opposite: the long process of construction itself undoubtedly contributed to the economic growth of the Netherlands, providing employment and incomes for many workers for many years.

Many proposals for clean energy and environmental protection emphasize the indirect benefits that these measures would provide.

For example, the Apollo Alliance, a coalition that includes many labor unions and environmental groups, has proposed a ten-point program for clean energy and jobs.[7] The Apollo program includes promotion of hybrid vehicles, public transportation, energy efficiency, renewable energy, and other measures. For a cost of $300 billion, it would eliminate 23 percent of US greenhouse gas emissions; in the process it would create an estimated 3.3 million new jobs, with massive employment increases in construction and manufacturing, and new incomes of more than four times the program's costs.

These indirect benefits could not occur in the abstract model of a competitive economy. In a perfectly competitive labor market, everyone who is willing and able to work already has a job that pays exactly what their labor is worth. Under those conditions, the Apollo program could only add 3.3 million new workers by paying higher wages to attract them away from other employers, thereby threatening to set off an inflationary spiral. Moreover, as seen in the last section, the theory of competitive markets tells us that there are no hugely profitable new opportunities to invest in clean energy lying on the sidewalk, because someone would have picked them up by now.

In the real world, unemployment happens. Many people are involuntarily out of work at times, or stuck in jobs where they produce and earn much less than they are capable of. When the economy is booming, there may not be 3.3 million workers with the needed skills available for new projects. In a recession, on the other hand, when more people are out of work, the employment boost provided by efforts like the Apollo program could be just what the country needs.

The focus on job creation recalls the economic theories of John Maynard Keynes. Seeking to understand the Great Depression of the 1930s, Keynes developed an analysis that explained why employment levels can vary, remaining far below full employment at times – and why government spending creates jobs indirectly in the private sector, as well as directly on public payrolls. Keynes's theory was widely accepted in academic economics from about 1940 to 1980. Its popularity waned in the increasingly conservative Reagan era and beyond, replaced by a revival of faith in unregulated market forces. However, news of the death of Keynesian economics has not yet reached state and municipal politicians, who often seem obsessed with job creation efforts in their jurisdictions. For elected officials, costs that create jobs for their constituents are good costs indeed.

An unrepentant Keynesian might observe that the US economy has never stopped relying on government spending to boost employment, but much of the spending, and the resulting job creation, has occurred through the military. Today the Soviet Union and the Cold War are long gone, leaving the Pentagon with many expensive weapon systems that are irrelevant to the radically changed world of the twenty-first century. So it should be possible to divert a large chunk of that government spending, replacing obsolete weapons with up-to-date defenses against the ominous new threat of climate change. If that happened, it would impose a cost on society, just like Pentagon spending, or Dutch investments in sea walls. The opportunity to pay that cost would be a cause for celebration.

Waiting for technology

In the long run, the deep reductions in carbon emissions needed for climate stabilization will require efforts beyond the scale of the Apollo program. The feasibility of a low-carbon future will ultimately depend on new technologies that have not yet been invented, or at best exist only in small, expensive prototypes. How much will it cost to invent, develop, and implement the low-carbon technologies we will need in the decades to come? Innovation is not a commodity, like steel or automobiles, which can be mass-produced in predictable quantities. Nonetheless, innovations do take place, and economies become more efficient over time.

The economic theory of competitive markets has little to say about technological change. If competition is already making the most productive possible use of labor and other resources, and maximizing the satisfaction of consumers, then what is the source of new technologies? A firm in a competitive market could not afford to undertake research and development unless it had immediate business applications.

Lacking a rigorous theory of innovation, economists have often assumed that new technologies simply appear, making the economy steadily more efficient over time. Specifically, in the context of energy and climate change, many models have assumed that there is a constant rate of "autonomous energy efficiency improvement" – that is, the ratio of energy use to GDP declines at a steady rate over time.[8] In effect, energy-saving innovations fall from the sky, without any expenditure of effort to create or adopt them.

The assumption of automatic, effortless technical progress not only sounds implausible; it leads directly to an unfortunate result. If the economy is becoming steadily less energy-intensive, and therefore less carbon-intensive, all the time, then waiting for future technological change to help solve the climate problem is an attractive strategy. If the long-run target is a fixed low level of emissions, it will be less expensive to get there if we start in a future year, when technology has already lowered emissions;

starting now would be more costly, since we would have to pay for emissions reductions that would otherwise come to us for free, if only we wait for them.

William Nordhaus refers to this strategy as the "climate policy ramp," starting slowly and only gradually climbing to more ambitious levels.[9] Nordhaus's climate economics model includes the assumption of automatic technical progress, making the policy ramp appear to be the best available choice. Ramping up slowly would be a credible option if technological progress were in fact automatic, and if there was no harm in waiting to solve the problem. However, neither premise is valid. There is abundant evidence of harm from waiting to address climate change, and useful innovations do not appear automatically.

Other economics research makes the common-sense point that innovations are often induced by government and business decisions. Some innovations involve a sudden breakthrough, a "eureka" moment; but many consist of small, cumulative improvements in existing processes. Costs of producing a new product typically decline as industry gains more experience with it, in a pattern called "learning by doing," or the "learning curve" effect. In a classic example from the early twentieth century, the cost of a Model T Ford dropped by 15 percent every time the cumulative production of Model Ts (counting from the beginning of the model run) doubled.[10] Similar patterns have been found in many products, although with varying rates of cost reduction.

Because the costs of new products decline as the volume of production grows, government policy can influence the pace and direction of technical change. In the 1970s, wind power was an impractical, expensive way to produce electricity. It was initially supported in the US by the federal government and the state of

California, and then developed further by Denmark, Germany, and other European countries. After thirty years of public support for its development, wind power is now cheap enough to compete with other sources of electricity in suitably windy areas. As this example suggests, financial support for early stages of research and development, followed by government purchases along with incentives for private buyers, can determine which potential innovations are commercialized and produced in large enough volume to become affordable. Other renewable energy sources and energy conservation technologies will need the same kind of public support to become cost-effective parts of the solution to climate change.

The previous section suggested that government policy has always affected employment, often through military spending. The same is true for technology. The US has funded the development of numerous innovative weapon systems, technologies that would not have automatically appeared without government support. Most of them, fortunately, have never been used. Along the way, many other technologies have been developed, with more peaceful applications to civilian life. In the words of a history of microelectronics,

> The U.S. military initially purchased nearly the total production of transistors in the early 1950's, using them to make the new generation of communications, radar and improved avionics systems, command and control systems, as well as for missiles and jet fighters...
>
> The U.S. government acted as the major market for integrated circuits in the early years... In 1962 ... the U.S. government, with extensive research interests in space, defense, and other areas, purchased virtually 100 percent of all integrated circuits manufactured in the United States.[11]

As with wind power, a few decades of generous public support were sufficient to launch the microelectronics industry as a success in the marketplace. And the list goes on and on: computers got their start with military purchases; the Internet grew out of ARPANET, a Defense Department-sponsored network set up in the 1960s to connect military researchers around the country.

None of these technologies appeared automatically. With an "electronics policy ramp," telling the public sector to start slowly on electronics investment, microelectronics might never have happened. Instead, the US government moved rapidly, and succeeded in launching a suite of technologies that now dominate private markets and shape modern life.

The Pentagon's success in jump-starting the microelectronics industry is a nearly great model for the development of climate-friendly technologies. We just have to do it again, but without building weapons. After all, the objective of climate policy is not to kill people, but to keep them alive. With technology creation, as with job creation, the military offers ample evidence of the effectiveness of government spending. The challenge now is to spend it, equally effectively, on something different.

This chapter started by asking what it will cost to do something about climate change. While the costs of climate policy should be easier to quantify than the benefits, it turns out that judgments about economic theory permeate the discussion of costs. In the short run, are costless emissions reductions impossible, or are they the natural place to start? In the medium term, are all costs equally bad, or can we identify good costs that create jobs and other desirable indirect benefits? In the long run, will the needed technologies show up automatically at a predictable pace, or should we induce and promote them by public policy decisions?

Not much is left, therefore, of the hope that costs and benefits of climate policy could be expressed and compared in monetary terms.

Nonetheless, there are continual attempts to apply cost–benefit techniques to climate problems. The next two chapters review the worst and the best in recent work on cost–benefit analysis of climate change.

6

Hot, it's not:
climate economics according to Lomborg

Polar bears are good swimmers. A picture of a polar bear swimming in open water does not prove that the bear is in imminent danger of drowning.

The overnight freezing portrayed in the movie *The Day After Tomorrow* is unrealistic. Climate change could not literally happen at that speed.

Ambient temperature is just one of the factors that influence the spread of malaria. Lowering carbon emissions in order to limit temperature increases is not the fastest or most cost effective way to combat malaria.

These are three of the things that environmental skeptic Bjørn Lomborg wants you to know about climate change. All three are true. All three are responses to mass media oversimplifications of the threat of climate change. Such oversimplification is an important problem to address if you agree with Lomborg's premise that the world is in danger of exaggerating the importance of climate change and doing too much to combat it.

If he had confined himself to actual examples of oversimplification and exaggeration in climate change rhetoric, Lomborg could have written a short, useful article – perhaps making the point that it is unhelpful and unnecessary to overstate the case, since the real problems of climate change are serious enough. Unfortunately, Lomborg did not write that article, but instead stretched his story into a book-length claim that climate change is only a moderately serious problem, while the proposed remedies are all prohibitively expensive. Many other problems, in his view, are both more urgent and cheaper to solve. He deserves attention here because he is one of the most effective writers raising economic arguments against active climate policies.[1]

Lomborg has written on these themes before. In *The Skeptical Environmentalist*,[2] he attempted an across-the-board challenge to the conventional wisdom of impending environmental crisis, including a sweeping and unpersuasive critique of the IPCC analysis of climate change. Numerous responses by scientists appeared, critiquing and correcting the treatment of environmental science throughout *The Skeptical Environmentalist*.

Lomborg then organized the so-called "Copenhagen Consensus," a panel of eight economists who evaluated other economists' cost–benefit analyses of priorities for global development.[3] Climate change fared particularly badly in the final Copenhagen Consensus rankings, classified as the lowest priority among the issues under consideration.

In his latest book, *Cool It*, Lomborg tackles climate change again, starting with the same attitude and reaching the same conclusion. While Lomborg accepts that climate change is caused at least in part by human activity, he maintains that it is not nearly as serious as environmental "extremists" would have us believe. Sharply reducing emissions now, he thinks, would be horribly expensive, as shown by his estimates of the huge economic losses resulting from the Kyoto Protocol. Meanwhile, as the "Consensus" claimed, there are other, more immediate problems which can be addressed more cost-effectively. Ignoring climate change is therefore evidence of concern for future generations:

> I hope that in forty years we will not have to tell our kids that we went in for a long series of essentially unsuccessful command-and-control Kyotos that had little or no effect on the climate but left them poorer and less able to deal with the problems of the future.[4]

A comprehensive response to the treatment of climate science and economics in *Cool It* would require a very long essay. This chapter focuses on three specific areas: questions of accuracy, bias, and authority; cost–benefit analysis of climate change versus other priorities; and Lomborg's understanding of economics.

Whom can you trust?

In *Cool It*, as in his previous books, Lomborg adopts a voice of authority. He offers a definitive-sounding explanation of the climate problem for a nontechnical audience, identifies and summarizes recent research, and tells his readers whom to trust and whom to doubt. This claim of authority fails both because the book is riddled with inaccuracies, and because it displays a pervasive bias in its coverage and evaluations of climate issues.

To begin with, Lomborg has a weak grasp of some of the essential details, and gives little or no explanation of how he reached his surprising results. These may seem like small points, but they undermine the book's claim to provide precise, authoritative evaluations throughout the fields of climate science and economics. The following are just a few illustrations of Lomborg's repeated errors in the details of the climate story.

Early in *Cool It*, Lomborg says:

> In its "standard" future scenario, the IPCC predicts that the global temperature in 2100 will have risen on average 4.7°F from the current range.[5]

There is in fact no such thing as one standard IPCC scenario; rather, a range of scenarios, none of them privileged above the others, describe alternate possible futures. In the notes at the back of the book, Lomborg explains that the standard he is referring to is "A1B, described as the business-as-usual scenario."[6] All of the major IPCC scenarios, however, are business-as-usual projections under varying assumptions about the world. Lomborg cites just one source for his (mistaken) belief about the unique status of A1B. That source, a technical article on climate modeling, never mentions A1B, and provides no support for Lomborg's view.

In discussing the impact of carbon taxes, Lomborg says:

> the total present-day cost for a permanent one-dollar [per ton] CO_2 tax is estimated at more than \$11 billion. So we might want to think twice about cranking up the knob to a thirty-dollar CO_2 tax, which will cost almost \$7 trillion.[7]

Why should a \$30 tax cost more than 600 times as much as a \$1 tax? Are the two estimates from the same model, and referring to the same time period? If this lopsided contrast is not a mistake, it is badly in need of explanation. The notes to this passage contain no hint as to sources, offering just one short, ambiguous sentence: "This is about \$390 million per year."[8] That note *could* mean that in some unnamed model, a $1 tax imposes costs of $390 million a year, which would become $11 billion when extended for 28 years. If, in that model, a $30 tax imposes annual costs thirty times as large as the $1 tax, then the higher tax would only lead to a total cost of $7 trillion after about 600 years, an unusually long period of time for evaluating a tax policy.

In addition to the inaccuracies, *Cool It* presents a biased and incomplete picture of climate science. Lomborg appears concerned with documenting the book's completeness: the 164 pages of text are supported by 34 pages of notes and a 42 page bibliography with more than 500 entries. The bibliographic entries, however, include numerous news stories, non-academic websites, standard government reports and data sources, and articles from the *Encyclopedia Britannica*, as well as citations to the scientific and economic literature. And the academic sources that are cited display a persistent slant toward climate skepticism and inaction.

Table 6.1 presents the number of citations of selected authors. Lomborg has multiple citations to several well-known climate skeptics, but none to many of the best-known mainstream climate scientists. While stating in the text that there is no consensus on the relationship between hurricanes and climate change, Lomborg cites eleven works by Roger Pielke Jr., a leading researcher on one side of the debate, and none from Kerry Emanuel, a comparable figure on the other side. A similar bias appears in the treatment of economics, heavily favoring those whose analyses call for doing very little, while ignoring those whose analyses support doing a lot about climate change. This one-sided bibliography refutes Lomborg's claim to provide an authoritative summary of the state of knowledge about climate change.

Table 6.1 Lomborg's bibliography: selected authors and frequency of citation (works cited)

Well-known climate skeptics		Well-known climate scientists	
Indur Goklany	4	James Hansen	o
Richard Lindzen	2	John Holdren	o
Patrick Michaels	4	John Houghton	o
		James McCarthy	o
		Stephen Schneider	o
Leading scientist skeptical of link between hurricanes and climate change		Leading scientist whose work supports link between hurricanes and climate change	
Roger Pielke Jr.	11	Kerry Emanuel	o
Economists whose work supports slow, small-scale responses to climate change		Economists whose work supports rapid, large-scale responses to climate change	
Richard Mendelsohn	2	Terry Barker	o
William Nordhaus	11	William Cline	o
Robert Stavins	1	Stephen DeCanio	o
Richard Tol	13	Chris Hope	o
Gary Yohe	4	Richard Howarth	o
		Claudia Kemfert	o

Note: Two works co-authored by Tol and Yohe are counted under each author, as is one work co-authored by Goklany and Lindzen.

Costs, benefits, and consensus

A mantra repeated throughout *Cool It* is the belief that other problems are more urgent than climate change, and more cost-effective
to address. Cost–benefit analyses of a range of competing priorities,
assembled in an earlier book about Lomborg's "Copenhagen Consensus" and cited frequently in the newer book, form the basis for
this belief. That consensus was reached among eight like-minded
economists, sitting in judgment on cost–benefit analyses performed
by a few dozen other economists. As Lomborg modestly describes
it, "A panel of top level economists, including four Nobel laureates,
then made the first explicit global priority list ever."[9]

One fundamental problem with cost–benefit analysis of climate
change was noted in Chapter 4: there are no meaningful monetary
valuations for many of the benefits of climate mitigation. There are,
in addition, two specific problems with the Copenhagen Consensus
application of cost–benefit methods: the range of policy options
considered by the "consensus" was arbitrarily truncated; and the
calculations in the "consensus" cost–benefit analyses rely heavily
on wishful thinking.

In the Copenhagen Consensus, climate change mitigation was
weighed against policies to address disease, malnutrition, and scat-
tered other problems. In addition, reducing barriers to free trade
somehow made it onto the list. The option of reducing US military
spending, on the other hand, was overlooked by the assembled
economists, although they did evaluate efforts to limit civil wars
in Africa.

But what public policy choice does their deliberation correspond
to? There is no fixed sum of money available for combating climate
change, disease, malnutrition, barriers to free trade, civil wars in

Africa and the other Copenhagen Consensus options. The policies they considered are not the only things that governments spend money on, nor are they the only ways in which rich countries affect poor people in developing nations. "Which do you prefer, climate change mitigation or AIDS prevention?" is a trick question, to which the answer should be that you don't have to choose. In the US, imagine how much progress on *all* the "consensus" issues could be made with the hundreds of billions of dollars spent each year by the Pentagon. Or one could equally well favor reducing farm subsidies or tax breaks for energy companies; or rolling back some of the recent, generous tax cuts for the rich; or any number of other modifications to government spending priorities and tax laws. The point is that the funding available for climate initiatives depends on political decisions in the US and other rich countries, not on the technicalities of cost–benefit analysis or the merits of assorted other policy options.

An additional problem is that the details of the Copenhagen Consensus cost–benefit analyses do not withstand scrutiny.[10] A different economist examined each policy, using methods of analysis that varied widely from one case to the next. Popular policies often received fantastically exaggerated benefit estimates, with little or no empirical support. A global program of AIDS prevention measures was said to have benefits worth fifty times its costs, based on optimistic extrapolation from experience with a pilot program; in contrast, malaria prevention had benefits worth "only" nineteen times its costs, based on experience with implementing large-scale programs. On the basis of these numbers, the Copenhagen Consensus judged AIDS prevention to be a higher priority than malaria prevention. Removal of trade barriers was assumed to produce a huge boost in developing-country growth rates – and that gain was assumed (without evidence) to continue undiminished for forty-five years after trade liberalization. The epitome of this numerical puffery occurred when one nutrition program was estimated to produce total global benefits worth 200 times its costs. None of the local case studies supporting that summary figure had benefit-cost ratios greater than 84, and some were as low as 6.

The Copenhagen Consensus paper on climate change, by William Cline, was quite different in tone, attempting a more sober, rigorous cost–benefit analysis and resisting the temptation to award fantastic numbers to his favorite policies. Using a modified version of William Nordhaus's model, Cline found that benefit–cost ratios for several active climate mitigation scenarios ranged from 2 to 4. The other Copenhagen Consensus economists were dismissive of Cline's results, rejecting his 1.5 percent discount rate as implausibly low – and pointing out that his benefit–cost ratios were far below those claimed for the rival policy options. In *Cool It*, Lomborg cites one of the other "consensus" economists' critique of Cline, but not Cline's analysis itself.

Three hundred years of Kyoto

Climate science has been debated for years and is becoming well-known; climate economics may be less familiar terrain. Lomborg attempts to define the boundary of acceptable economic opinion, offering summary judgments about what "all" analysts believe:

> All major peer-reviewed economic models agree that little emissions reduction is justified. A central conclusion from a meeting of all economic modelers was: "Current assessments determine that the 'optimal' policy calls for a relatively modest level of control of CO_2."[11]

The meeting in question was a workshop of nineteen people, not all of them economic modelers, held in 1996.

The attempted demarcation of the boundaries of "all" economic thought merges with Lomborg's reverent attitude toward Richard Tol, the most frequently cited author in the bibliography. Tol is described as having written "the biggest review article of all the literature's" estimates of the social cost of carbon, i.e. the monetary value of the damages done by emitting one more ton of CO_2.[12] But Tol has done much more than writing the biggest article; as Lomborg explains:

> When I specifically asked him [Tol] for his best guess, he wasn't too enthusiastic about shedding his cautiousness – true researchers invariably are this way – but gave a best estimate of two dollars per ton. This means that the damage we will cause by putting out one more ton of CO_2 is likely two dollars. ... If we tax it at $85, as proposed in one radical report, while the real damage is two dollars, we lose up to $83 of social benefits.[13]

From this passage in the text, the reader has to consult both the notes and the bibliography in the back to find that the "radical report" in question is the Stern Review, published in Britain by that notorious radical organization, Her Majesty's Treasury. The thoughtful, extensively researched Stern Review (discussed in Chapter 7) comes in for extended criticism from Lomborg, while Tol's previously unpublished – and astonishingly low – personal guess at the social cost of carbon is simply pronounced correct: "We should tax CO_2 at the economically correct level of about two dollars per ton."[14]

In Lomborg's view, it is not only Tol who speaks for the economics profession as a whole. Several statements about "the models" as a whole are documented only with citations to a single model

developed by Lomborg's other favorite economist, William Nordhaus. Likewise, Nordhaus is the only economist cited in support
of a discussion of the vast cost of the Kyoto Protocol over the next
century and more.[15] The long time span may surprise those who
recall that the Kyoto Protocol extends only to 2012. Nordhaus,
however, has invented what he describes as the "Kyoto forever"
scenario, in which the provisions of the Kyoto Protocol are extended
indefinitely – allowing the attribution of many years' worth of costs
to this short-term proposal.[16]

A widely quoted Nordhaus estimate is that the Kyoto Protocol
would impose global costs of $716 billion; the original study shows
that this is the present value of 300 years of "Kyoto forever," assuming that carbon emissions trading occurs only among industrial
countries.[17] This seemingly large total is less than $2.5 billion per
year over the 300-year span, not even 40¢ per person per year at the
world's current population. The same study, moreover, shows that
if global emissions trading is allowed, the 300-year total cost drops
to a present value of only $59 billion, equivalent to $0.2 billion per
year, or less than 3¢ per person per year. Thus if the world were
to do something as utterly bizarre and inconceivable as extending
the Kyoto Protocol unchanged for 300 years, and if Nordhaus were
correct about the resulting costs, almost all of the costs could be
avoided by introducing global emissions trading.

Despite Lomborg's certainty about what "all" economics looks
like, Nordhaus, Tol, and like-minded researchers do not represent
the whole of the economics profession. The Stern Review and the
work of the economists in the right-hand column of Table 6.1,
above, provide important examples of alternatives – and there are
many more. There are numerous published estimates of the costs
of the Kyoto Protocol, most of them by economists who somehow

missed the 1996 workshop of "all" modelers – and failed, as well, to be mentioned in *Cool It*.

Lomborg's suggestion that all economic models produce more or less the same results is dead wrong; in fact, estimates of Kyoto costs have differed so widely that there have been three meta-analyses seeking to explain the sources of disagreement.[18] Factors such as the extent of emissions trading, the uses of government carbon tax or permit auction revenues, the treatment of co-benefits of carbon reduction, and several technical assumptions about economic modeling turn out to have major impacts on the estimated costs. One of the meta-analyses, focusing on costs to the United States, concluded that if policies implementing the Kyoto Protocol were "expected, gradual, and well designed," the net costs of mitigation for the US would be insignificant.[19]

Bjørn Lomborg was a political scientist with limited research experience, none of it in economics, before he turned to a career in environmental skepticism. He misrepresents many thoughtful, hard-working economists by his claim that the entire profession supports his opposition to active, large-scale climate policies. His lopsided choice of sources and misleading collection of quotes and assertions provide a caricature of economics at its worst, wielding a narrow cost–benefit analysis as a weapon against common sense and scientific evidence.

Not everyone who uses traditional economic arguments and methods comes up with the same answers as Lomborg. Following this look at the worst of conventional climate economics, the next chapter turns to the best that has been done with similar techniques, in the Stern Review.

7

Much less wrong:
the Stern Review versus its critics

In 2005, British chancellor of the exchequer Gordon Brown (who later became prime minister) asked Sir Nicholas Stern to conduct a major review of the economics of climate change, as a guide to developing government policy. Stern had previously been the chief economist at the World Bank and a prominent figure in the British government. It is not a background that suggested he would make radical new departures in his report.

Yet the Stern Review, released in 2006, expressed alarm at the impending climate damages that will result from business as usual, and presented novel economic arguments endorsing prompt and vigorous action.[1] Other economists were quick to respond, often quite critically. How could Stern have strayed so far from traditional economic analyses, which tend to recommend much smaller and slower responses? Stern was accused of numerous violations of standard economic methodology, which supposedly led to his "errors."

This chapter reviews the differences between Stern and his critics.[2] While the Stern Review is not a perfect document, it rests on much sounder ground than the work of many of the economists who have attacked it. It illustrates important ways in which economic analysis can reflect the urgency of the climate problem – even though it ultimately offers incomplete solutions to some important aspects of the problem. Indeed, most of the criticism has been pointed in the wrong direction: if anything, Stern understated the threat of climate change, and missed some of the strongest arguments for immediate action.

What did Stern conclude?

"The scientific evidence is now overwhelming: climate change presents very serious global risks, and it demands an urgent global response. ... The benefits of strong, early action considerably outweigh the costs."[3] This central conclusion from the Stern Review will not come as a surprise to many scientists who study climate change. But in the world of economics, it was so unusual that it required detailed justification.

Stern found that under business-as-usual conditions (i.e. assuming no new policies to reduce carbon emissions), the concentration of greenhouse gases in the atmosphere could reach double the pre-industrial level as early as 2035. This would essentially commit the world to more than 2°C (3.6°F) of warming. By the end of the century, business as usual would lead to more than a 50 percent chance of exceeding 5°C (9°F) of warming, implying disastrous changes in natural ecosystems and human living conditions around the world.

Stern described the impacts of unchecked warming in both qualitative and quantitative terms; the qualitative images are perhaps more sweeping and powerful. For example, human actions create "risks of major disruption to economic and social activity, on a scale similar to those associated with the great wars and the economic depression of the first half of the twentieth century."[4] (American readers should remember that this was written in a country that was hit much harder than the US by World Wars I and II.[5]) An average global warming of 5°C (9°F) would cause "a radical change in the physical geography of the world [that] must lead to major changes in the human geography – where people live and how they live their lives."[6]

Most of the economic debate, however, concerns Stern's quantitative estimates. The economic model used in the Stern Review finds that the climate damages from business as usual would be expected to reduce GDP by 5 percent based on market impacts alone, or 11 percent including a rough estimate for the value of health and environmental effects that do not have market prices ("externalities," in the jargon of economics; see Chapter 1). If the sensitivity of climate to CO_2 levels turns out to be higher than the baseline estimates, these losses could rise to 7 percent and more than 14 percent, respectively. Stern speculates that an adjustment for equity weighting, reflecting the fact that the impacts will fall most heavily on poor countries (see Chapter 8), could lead to losses valued at 20 percent of global GDP. These figures are substantially greater than the comparable estimates from many other economists.

These damages can be largely avoided, according to Stern, at moderate cost through emissions reduction. Stabilization at 450–550 parts per million (ppm) of CO_2 equivalent[7] in the atmosphere would avoid most, though not all, of the business-as-usual damages.

Several methods of estimation suggest that stabilization at this level would cost about 1 percent of GDP. Stabilization below 450 ppm, according to Stern, is no longer economically feasible in view of the large amount of carbon already in the atmosphere; so in his view, the relevant range of targets is now 450–550 ppm of CO_2 equivalent.[8]

The extensive published criticisms raise three principal points, claiming that the Stern Review:

- used too low a discount rate;
- treated risk and uncertainty inappropriately;
- calculated and compared costs and benefits incorrectly.

A fourth point, suggested by only a few of the comments, deserves more attention: does Stern's quantitative analysis actually understate the severity of the problem? The following sections of this chapter address each of the four points in turn.

Is the Stern discount rate too low?

As explained in Chapter 2, the discount rate is decisive for climate economics, because the climate impacts of today's decisions span such long periods of time. Stern's preferred discount rate, 1.4 percent, is much lower than the rates used in traditional climate economic models. For William Nordhaus, "the *Review*'s radical view of policy stems from an extreme assumption about discounting … this magnifies impacts in the distant future and rationalizes deep cuts in emissions, and indeed in all consumption, today."[9]

Recall from Chapter 2 that there are two components of the discount rate. The *rate of pure time preference* is the discount rate that should apply if all present and future generations had equal resources. The *wealth-based component* of the discount rate reflects the assumption that if future generations will be richer than we are, then there is less need for us to invest today in order to help them protect themselves.

Stern reviewed and endorsed the philosophical arguments for viewing all generations as people of equal worth, deserving equal rights and living conditions. As the Review put it, "if you care little about future generations you will care little about climate change. As we have argued that is not a position which has much foundation in ethics ... [It is a position] which many would find unacceptable."[10] To quantify an ethical perspective that respects and validates the future, it is necessary to set pure time preference close to zero.

Nordhaus, like many economists, believes that people reveal their time preferences through choices about savings and other actions affecting the future, and deduces from this that the rate of pure time preference must be significantly greater than zero. In contrast, Stern could be described as setting pure time preference trivially greater than zero. Stern observed that a natural or man-made disaster could destroy the human race; he arbitrarily assumed the probability of such a disaster to be 0.1 percent per year, and set pure time preference at that rate. That is, Stern assumed that we are only 99.9 percent sure that humanity will still be here next year, so we should consider the well-being of people next year to be 99.9 percent as important as people today.

Stern also assumed that the wealth-related component of the discount rate should match the growth of per capita income, which he projected at an average of 1.3 percent per year. Thus his combined discount rate was 1.4 percent.

In objecting to Stern's choice of a discount rate, Nordhaus relied on another idea from economic theory: in an abstractly perfect market economy, the discount rate would match market interest rates. Based on this theory, Nordhaus maintained that the discount rate should match an interest rate of about 5 percent. This theory and its limitations were introduced in Chapter 2.[11] Briefly, the argument that discount rates should match current interest rates is grounded in hypothetical, perfect markets, not in reality. In the actually existing market economy, interest rates reflect the short-run private decisions of those who can afford to participate in financial markets today, not public decisions about intergenerational ethics.

Another economist, Partha Dasgupta, presented a complementary critique of Stern, addressing the wealth-related component of the discount rate.[12] He interpreted the wealth-related component as a measure of the trade-off between rich and poor, independent of time differences. Dasgupta endorsed Stern's argument that pure time preference is close to zero, but maintained that equity requires much more concern for the poor, now and in the future. This would be reflected in a larger wealth-related component of the discount rate. If per capita incomes are expected to continue growing, as most economists (including Stern) assume, then a larger wealth-related component leads to a higher overall discount rate, and indirectly to less investment in the future.

How can a concern for equity lead to doing less for future generations? The source of the paradox is the assumption that future generations will be better off than we are; in this story, we are the poor, and those who come after us are the rich. If that were true, then as modern Robin Hoods we could strike a blow for equality by taking money from our children's inheritance and spending it on ourselves today. On the other hand, if climate change or other problems will make future generations worse off, the argument reverses: in that case, the present generation should do much more for its poorer descendants. Dasgupta has raised this possibility in other writings on the subject.

In summary, Stern makes many valid arguments about discount rates, but these do not necessarily support his precise numbers; it is hard to be confident of the 0.1 percent annual risk of global catastrophe, an admittedly arbitrary estimate. The 1.3 percent average growth rate of per capita consumption is possible but far from certain to occur. A balanced conclusion might be that Stern demonstrates that 1.4 percent is among the plausible discount rates – and that such low rates have profoundly different implications from rates like 5–6 percent, used in many other analyses.

How do risk and uncertainty affect climate economics?

The second major innovation in the Stern analysis is the treatment of risk and uncertainty connected to climate change. This is the problem addressed in Chapter 3: although the broad outlines and major findings of climate science are increasingly definite, many crucial details remain uncertain, and may not be known until it is too late to do anything about the problem.

Stern introduced uncertainty into his economic calculations in three ways.[13] The first involves the sensitivity of climate to greenhouse gas concentrations – i.e., the climate sensitivity parameter, discussed in Chapter 3. Stern's baseline scenario follows the IPCC's 2001 report in assuming that a doubling of pre-industrial CO_2 concentrations would lead to warming of 1.5–4.5°C. Since subsequent research suggests that climate feedback mechanisms may increase sensitivity beyond that level, Stern includes a high climate sensitivity scenario that assumes that a doubling of atmospheric CO_2 would lead to warming of 2.4–5.4°C.

Second, the computer model used in the Stern Review includes an estimate for the risk of an abrupt climate catastrophe. The model assumes that once a threshold temperature is reached (the threshold itself is uncertain, but averages 5°C above pre-industrial temperatures) the probability of catastrophe increases by 10 percent for every additional degree of warming; the catastrophe, if it occurs, reduces output by an uncertain amount in the range of 5–20 percent.[14] As Stern notes, this feature of his model is based on the treatment of catastrophe in Nordhaus's model; most other economic models do not include any estimates for catastrophic events.

Finally, the Stern model is designed to reflect risks throughout its calculations, through the statistical technique known as Monte Carlo analysis. For 31 key parameters, the model assumes that the true value is unknown, but there is a range of possible values; the temperature threshold for catastrophes is an example of one of those uncertain parameters. For each of these parameters, the model randomly selects a value from the range of possibilities, each time it is run. The model is run repeatedly – 1,000 times, in this case – and an average of the results is used as the model's estimate.

Each of these three methods of modeling uncertainty has an important influence on the results. Yet despite its importance and its methodological innovation, the Stern treatment of uncertainty has received relatively little attention from economists. In a comment on Stern's treatment of catastrophic damages, Paul Baer argues that greater catastrophic impacts should have been included, starting at lower temperatures.[15] Stern's target for climate stabilization, according to Baer, should entail significant risks of the complete melting of the Greenland ice sheet, an important, much-discussed example of a climate catastrophe. Based on the risk of catastrophic damages at lower temperatures, Baer speculates that the optimal target for CO_2 reduction and temperature stabilization should be lower than Stern's levels.

Martin Weitzman, whose theory of uncertainty was discussed in Chapter 3, describes Stern as being "right for the wrong reason,"[16] because Stern places too much emphasis on a debatable cost–benefit analysis and too little on the need for social insurance against low-probability, catastrophic events. Weitzman's theory of uncertainty implies that we should worry less about calibrating the most likely outcomes, and more about insurance against worst-case catastrophes. Those potential catastrophes are far worse than the modest estimate for catastrophic losses used by Stern.

As with discount rates, it is safer to interpret the Stern results as showing that reasonable guesses about uncertainty can have a big effect on the bottom line, rather than attempting to defend the details of his results. Indeed, Baer argues in a specific case, and Weitzman demonstrates in theoretical terms, that uncertainties and catastrophic risks may be more serious and decisive than Stern recognizes. Stern's valuation of a climate catastrophe, built on Nordhaus estimates from some years ago (which in turn were originally based on an early poll of climate experts' best guesses[17]), seems likely to be an understatement. The Monte Carlo analysis, with 31 parameters allowed to vary, provides an insightful, graphic illustration of the effects of uncertainty in many corners of the model; but is it believable that the modelers know the probability distributions for all 31 parameters with any certainty? The deep uncertainty identified by Weitzman, and discussed in Chapter 3, is more than any existing computer model can convey – even a relatively creative model, such as Stern's, which attempts to reflect the impact of uncertainty.

How should damages and
mitigation costs be estimated?

Numerous economists have criticized Stern's estimates of costs and benefits. When it comes to estimating climate damages, Richard Tol and Gary Yohe believe that Stern has exaggerated throughout: "The *Stern Review* consistently selects the most pessimistic study in the literature for water, agriculture, health, and insurance."[18] Robert Mendelsohn adds the claim that Stern has overstated the effects and the certainty of extreme weather events, and has downplayed the likely extent of adaptation to a changing climate. Mendelsohn believes that the early stages of warming will be beneficial, particularly in agriculture (see Chapter 4); as a result, "there are hardly any damages associated with a 2°C increase in temperature."[19] The ever-imaginative Bjørn Lomborg reveals that Stern's damage estimates are inflated because "he assumes that we will continue to pump out carbon far into the 22nd century – a rather unlikely scenario given the falling cost of alternative fuels."[20]

There are also criticisms of the manner in which the Stern Review compares costs and benefits. Tol and Yohe express surprise that although Stern's marginal damage cost estimate is three times the previous British government estimate, his target for stabilizing greenhouse gas emissions is unchanged from the previous policy. If damages are so much higher, why isn't the stabilization target lower? On the other hand, Mendelsohn thinks that Stern should have explored the costs and benefits of higher stabilization targets, such as 650 or 750 ppm; from Mendelsohn's perspective, these targets might be the optimal ones to aim for.

Stern and his colleagues have responded to many of their critics on their website and in academic articles. The Stern Review damage estimate of 5 percent of GDP is based on the science in the IPCC's Third Assessment Report (2001). It is higher than other estimates as a result of the lower discount rate applied to future damages, the expanded treatment of uncertainty, and the enormous impact of the risk of 5°c or more warming within the 200-year time frame of the study. Many other studies focus on the important, but much smaller, damages expected from 2–3°c of warming.

Despite the thoroughness of the research that went into the Stern Review, there is one outstanding puzzle about the cost–benefit comparison, involving the narrow range of plausible targets. Stabilization at less than 450 ppm of CO_2 equivalent is no longer possible at affordable cost, according to Stern, while anything above 550 ppm is too dangerous to consider. This pattern is hard to understand; Baer, as well as Tol and Yohe, objects that Stern's account of damages should lead to a lower stabilization target.

To support Stern's narrow window, one would have to assume that mitigation costs become intolerably large for stabilization just below 450 ppm, while climate damages become intolerably large just above 550 ppm. This is a logically possible picture of the world, but it does not appear certain – and Stern has not provided a persuasive argument on either end of the range.

Did Stern underestimate the problem?

Finally, consider the possibility that Stern's error lies in the opposite direction from the majority of the economic criticism: do the Stern model estimates underestimate the severity of the climate problem? This is suggested in the discussion of uncertainty by both Baer and Weitzman, and indirectly by Tol and Yohe's comments on the stabilization targets.

Another limitation, overlooked in the initial debate, is that the Stern estimates of damages assume substantial, nearly costless adaptation will occur in developed countries. This issue arose in a study of climate damages for the US, in which Elizabeth Stanton and I collaborated with Chris Hope, the Cambridge University economist who developed the model used by Stern.[21] The Stern Review's estimate of US climate damages is only 0.4 percent of GDP by 2100.[22] One would expect US damages to be lower, in percentage terms, than the global average, since the US is colder than many countries and has a smaller than average fraction of its population and economic activity in low-lying coastal areas that are vulnerable to sea-level rise. Nonetheless, the Stern estimates for the US seem surprisingly low. Hope explained that the Stern estimates for developed countries consist of damages remaining after the assumed (successful, low-cost) adaptation effort.

For our analysis, Hope reran the model with three changes: he eliminated all adaptation assumptions, responded to Baer's critique by lowering the threshold at which catastrophes become possible, and increased the sensitivity of non-catastrophic damages to rising temperatures. The result is that business-as-usual climate damages will amount to an estimated loss of 1.5 percent of US GDP by 2100, prior to any adaptation. Within the modeling framework of the Stern Review, higher figures along these lines give a more appropriate estimate of damages (prior to adaptation). Similar changes applied to the Stern analysis of global damages would lead to larger estimates, arguing for a lower stabilization target and larger, faster policy responses.

A deeper question concerns the modeling framework itself. Does any version of monetary damage estimates, expressed as losses of a fraction of per capita consumption, actually convey the seriousness of the problem? As David Maddison observed, Stern's estimate of a 1.3 percent long-term annual growth in real per capita consumption implies that in 2200, without climate damages, the world would be 12.3 times as rich as today.[23] In that scenario, even if there is a 35 percent reduction in consumption due to climate change, an estimate mentioned in the Stern Review for an extreme worst-case scenario, the world of 2200 would be "only" 8.0 times as rich as today. This hardly sounds like a measure of worrisome harms.

Consider the estimate of 20 percent loss of consumption, offered by the Review as the likely value for the high climate sensitivity scenario with catastrophic risk, non-market damages, and an equity adjustment thrown in. Over the 200-year span of the Stern analysis, in the context of a steadily growing economy, a 20 percent loss is essentially an insignificant perturbation. If the long-term growth rate is reduced by 0.11 percentage points – cutting Stern's 1.3 percent annual growth to 1.19 percent per year, for example – then after 200 years, output will be reduced by 20 percent.

Alternatively, a 20 percent reduction could be the result of a brief interruption in growth, followed by resuming at the same rate as before. After a period of rapid growth, the Japanese economy experienced a decade of stagnation in the 1990s, with growth rates averaging more than two percentage points below the level of the 1980s.[24] More recently Japan has begun to grow again. Suppose that Japan were to resume the growth rate of the 1980s and maintain it unchanged for the next 200 years. Under that assumption, the macroeconomic problems of the 1990s would have caused Japan to lose 20 percent of the consumption that would otherwise have been available, throughout the 200-year period. In a faster-growing country such as China, which has reached 10 percent annual growth rates, a 20 percent permanent loss of consumption could result from a mere two-year pause, followed by resumption of long-term rapid growth.

Neither Japan's lost decade of growth in the 1990s, nor an imaginary two-year hiatus in China's faster growth, represents a qualitative disaster for the societies involved. No great loss of life, or of a way of life, is involved. To return to Stern's evocative metaphor, the impacts of World War II on Japan and China were of an entirely different nature and magnitude. There were, of course, vast, economically important wartime losses of property and income. But it is difficult to imagine any single monetary estimate that conveys the qualitative impact of a major war. If the expected impact of climate change resembles the effects of the great wars of the twentieth century, then it does not look like a mere 20 percent loss of consumption in a steadily growing economy.

The problem is not just that 20 percent is too small a loss. It is inevitably difficult to summarize a climate catastrophe with a single number, such as a percentage reduction in consumption. The profundity of human and ecological loss implied in the portraits of climate change, especially at higher temperatures, is only cheapened and diminished by pretending that all of it has a price. At the depths of greatest tragedy, as at the heights of proudest collective response, we leave the market far behind. The reason to avoid another world war is not primarily because repairing bombed-out buildings is so costly. The urgency of preparing wisely in advance for two, three, many Hurricane Katrinas is not strengthened by a hypothetical monetary valuation of the lives lost to the storm in 2005. Our moral obligation to protect the lives and livelihoods of future generations is not adequately conveyed by a numerical discount rate – even a low one. How could any estimate of the social cost of carbon bring these overarching ethical concerns back into the calculus of the marketplace, telling us precisely how to think and how much to care about our responsibilities to society, nature, and future generations?

The Stern Review is far from being the last word on the economics of climate change – but it is much less wrong than many of the analyses that preceded it. Stern's provocative analysis has decisively laid to rest the notion that standard economic methods necessarily counsel timidity in the face of global crisis.

8

Climate, equity, and development

Much of the climate policy debate is couched in national or regional terms. Yet the climate crisis is caused by worldwide carbon emissions, and cannot be solved in one place at a time. Whether or not we think locally, we will have to act globally to rescue the atmosphere and protect our common future.

That global effort will involve spending quite a bit of money. The "no-regrets" emissions reductions and energy savings, discussed in Chapter 5, will provide helpful first steps. However, the no-regrets options alone are not nearly enough to finish the job; there will be ample opportunities for regrets when the bills come due.

To reach a global climate agreement, it will be necessary to decide on each country's share of the costs. The Kyoto Protocol, the first major international agreement, developed a formula referred to as "common but differentiated responsibilities": it specified emissions reductions that had to be achieved by industrial countries by 2008–2012, averaging roughly 5 percent below their 1990 emissions.[1]

The countries that were subject to this requirement were listed in the Kyoto Protocol's Annex I, a term that became part of the language of negotiation. Non-Annex I (i.e. developing) countries were not included until after 2012, when a new round of reductions was expected to begin.

The US government refused to sign the Kyoto Protocol, maintaining that it was unfair to place the entire burden on the Annex I countries while allowing major carbon emitters such as China and India to escape from any costs or responsibilities. Although the Kyoto Protocol was designed as a first step, intended to be followed by different steps in the near future, much of the US debate judged the Protocol as if it were a problematical model for long-term policy. (Recall Nordhaus's "Kyoto forever" scenario, from Chapter 6.)

As the world looks toward a post-Kyoto agreement for the years beyond 2012, the question arises again: What is an equitable basis for allocation of the global burden of climate protection? There are two major categories of answers: responsibility for reduction can be based either on some measure of emissions, or on some version of ability to pay. This chapter examines the implications of each category, then turns to a new proposal for international allocation of climate costs, and closes with a look at the political debate over economics and equity.

Responsibility based on emissions: should the polluters pay?

A basic notion of environmental justice is embodied in the "polluter pays" principle: those who profit from emitting pollution should pay for cleaning it up. On this principle, responsibility for the costs of reduction should be proportional to greenhouse gas emissions. There are several distinct variants on this idea, linking responsibility to differing measures and interpretations of emissions.

Most obviously, reductions could be based on current emissions (or, in practice, emissions in a recent year for which data are available). This is the approach the Kyoto Protocol adopted within Annex I: each country's required reductions were a percentage of the country's 1990 emissions. Nothing could be simpler than this approach; it is easy to understand and explain, and it uses readily available, relatively standardized and reliable data. There are, however, at least two other interpretations of emissions that could be used to set national responsibilities.

First, how should we count the greenhouse gases that are caused by production for export? If China burns coal to manufacture goods that are exported to the United States, are the resulting carbon dioxide emissions the responsibility of Chinese producers or American consumers? It seems appropriate, in the abstract, for consumers to bear the responsibility for pollution created in producing the goods they buy. In practice, however, the available data are organized by the location of emissions; it takes quite a bit of calculation to assign emissions to the ultimate consumers.

A number of academic studies have attempted to measure the pollution embodied in international trade. A common finding is that developed countries import more pollution-intensive goods than they export; in effect, they have shifted part of the pollution created by their consumption onto developing countries. In the case of carbon dioxide, the US, Japan, and all the largest European economies are net carbon importers, while China and many other developing countries, Russia, Australia, Canada, and (perhaps) some Scandinavian countries are net carbon exporters.[2] Thus allocating responsibility for emissions based on the location of consumption would increase the share of the global burden borne by the US, Japan, and the largest European countries, while decreasing the burden on many developing countries, and also on rich, resource-exporting countries.

My own contribution to this literature was an analysis of the carbon content of US–Japan trade, done in collaboration with Masanobu Ishikawa of Kobe University and Mikio Suga of Tokyo International University.[3] We found that the US was importing slightly more carbon from Japan than vice versa, but the net effect was less than one percent of each country's emissions. US imports from Japan are larger in volume but lower in carbon intensity than US exports to Japan, so the total amount of carbon embodied in trade is almost the same in both directions. Net carbon imports from the world as a whole were much bigger, around 4 percent of national emissions for both countries. Therefore, allocation of emissions based on the location of consumption rather than production would increase the emissions of both Japan and the US by roughly 4 percent.

A second interpretation bases responsibility for reductions on the history of emissions, rather than a single year. Carbon dioxide stays in the atmosphere for a long time, on average at least 100 years. The twentieth century's emissions are still contributing to the greenhouse effect – and, if we take carbon constraints seriously, preventing other countries from making equally free use of fossil fuels today. Perhaps, therefore, polluters should pay in proportion to their cumulative carbon emissions over a century or so.

As shown in Figure 8.1, calculation of emissions on a long-term cumulative basis would shift more responsibility onto the US and Europe.[4] India, with 17 percent of the world's population,

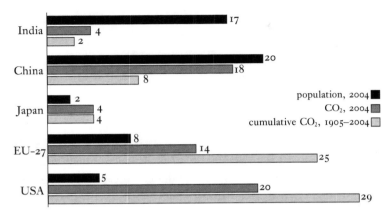

Figure 8.1   Shares of world population and CO_2 emissions, selected countries (% of world total)

Source: Climate Analysis Indicators Tool (CAIT) Version 5.0 (Washington DC: World Resources Institute, 2008), http://cait.wri.org. Emissions data used in this graph include only CO_2 emissions from fossil fuel combustion and cement production.

accounted for 4 percent of current (actually 2004) emissions, but only 2 percent over the century from 1905 to 2004. At the other extreme, the US, with 5 percent of global population, accounts for 20 percent of current and 29 percent of cumulative emissions. Japan became affluent only in the late twentieth century, and has less of a history of emissions than other rich countries; it accounts for about the same share, 4 percent, of global emissions on either a current or a cumulative basis.

The US, Europe, and Japan together represent 15 percent of the world's population, and are responsible for 38 percent of emissions on a current basis, but 58 percent on a 100-year cumulative basis. Thus a standard based on cumulative emissions would look quite different from one based on current emissions.

Responsibility based on income: should the rich pay?

Making the polluters pay – setting standards and allocating costs
based on some measure of emissions – is only one way to think
about fairness. Regardless of who is responsible for past or present
emissions levels, higher-income countries are more able to shoulder
the future economic burden of climate protection. How, if at all,
should income enter into the standards for sharing the global costs
of climate policy? Is it possible to assign responsibility in a way
that helps to equalize incomes, and thereby creates opportunities
for economic growth in developing countries?

One widely discussed policy proposal is known as "contraction
and convergence." It calls for an initial period of convergence to
equal per capita carbon emission allowances around the world,
followed by a gradual contraction of the allowances over time until
a sustainable level of carbon emissions is reached. Countries that
wanted to emit more than their allowances would have to buy
emission rights from those countries – generally lower-income
ones – that did not need all of their allowances. Such purchases
could create a substantial flow of money to the countries most in
need of development. The contraction and convergence proposal
is based on a simple, appealing principle of international equity,
and has been endorsed by many developing countries, as well as a
number of politicians and organizations in developed countries.

However, there is no visible movement toward adopting contraction and convergence, or any other form of equal per capita
emission rights – perhaps because the allowances would be so
far below current emissions in many countries. According to one
advocate, contraction and convergence would imply an initial
allowance of 7 tons of carbon dioxide per person per year, and

would have to contract to 2 tons per person by later in this century.[5]

Current emissions (meaning, as in Figure 8.1, CO_2 emissions for 2004) are 20 tons per person in the US, and 10 tons per person in Germany and Japan.[6] An allowance of 7 tons per capita matches the current emission level in some of the poorest parts of Europe, such as Serbia, Ukraine, and Belarus. Some richer countries that rely heavily on nuclear power and/or hydroelectric power (i.e. ways of producing electricity without carbon emissions) also stay under 7 tons per capita; France and Sweden are notable examples.

A longer-term cap of 2 tons of carbon dioxide per person corresponds to a point even farther down the world income distribution; it is the current emissions level of Egypt or Brazil. It would require about a 50 percent cut in emissions for China, Argentina, Chile, and Mexico, all of which currently emit about 4 tons of carbon dioxide per person. With a cap at 2 tons, per capita carbon dioxide emissions could still almost double in countries such as India, the Philippines, Peru, and Vietnam, and could triple in Nigeria. Nevertheless, those countries would hit the carbon ceiling long before they reached the level of China or Mexico today.

By way of comparison, another widely discussed target, 80 percent reduction in emissions by 2050, would mean 4 tons per person in the US if the population remained constant. Since the US population is growing but the emissions target is not, 80 percent reduction by 2050 will actually mean less than 3 tons per capita for the US, not much above the 2 ton standard under contraction and convergence.

Even 2 tons per person may not be low enough for the long run; many scenarios for climate stabilization call for reaching that level around mid-century and continuing with further reductions.

There is only a limited amount of space in the atmosphere for greenhouse gas emissions, and most of that space has already been used up by the past emissions of today's rich countries. So a formula of equal per capita emission rights, combined with an emissions cap set low enough to avoid a climate catastrophe, allows very little opportunity for development. If the link between carbon emissions and development remains as strong as it has been in the past, then there is almost no remaining space for sustainable development, regardless of who gets the emission rights. To make climate protection compatible with development it will be necessary to create new, low-carbon pathways to economic growth.

Greenhouse development rights

The challenges facing the next international climate agreement are complex: low-income countries need some assurance that they will have opportunities for development despite carbon constraints, while high-income countries need to know that everyone who is able to do so is sharing the costs of climate protection.

A provocative recent proposal addresses the dilemmas of climate and development through the calculation of "greenhouse development rights," based on both emissions and income.[7] The authors, Paul Baer, Tom Athanasiou, and Sivan Kartha, emphasize that it is too late to talk about emission rights as a path to development. If carbon emissions from industrial countries magically fell to zero tomorrow, while developing countries followed the slowest-growing of the IPCC's business-as-usual scenarios (B1), the world would still hit the carbon ceiling and face the need to begin reducing emissions before 2030. The only reasonable response is to launch an emergency program to reduce carbon emissions and create low-carbon technologies worldwide, and to distribute the costs of that emergency program in a manner that protects the right to development.

Baer, Athanasiou, and Kartha (BAK, for short) propose that the right to development consists of being exempt from sharing the costs of climate protection until you are above a global poverty line; they recommend $9,000 per person per year, measured in purchasing power terms. This is just above the world average income; it is close to the average income of Brazil, Bulgaria, Romania, and Thailand. For BAK, the right to development is based on individual incomes, not national averages: people above the poverty threshold in India are responsible for a share of the global climate costs, and people below the threshold in the US are not. Specifically, they find that 5 percent of the population of India, 20 percent of China, 90 percent of the US, 97 percent of Japan, and 98 to 100 percent of most northern European countries are above the threshold.

For each country, BAK estimate both the capacity to share the global climate costs and the responsibility for climate change. The calculation of capacity resembles an income tax with a personal exemption of $9,000. Your income above that level, if any, is your personal slice of the global capacity to pay for carbon reduction. Under this formula, capacity rises faster than income: at $20,000, your capacity is $11,000; double your income, to $40,000, and your capacity almost triples, to $31,000.

Responsibility is based on cumulative emissions since 1990, because, according to BAK, it was well known by then that greenhouse gas emissions were contributing to climate change. However, the historical emissions resulting from producing each person's first $9,000 of income are excluded, exactly as with the capacity calculation.

The cost-sharing formula is a weighted average of capacity and responsibility, giving greater weight to capacity. Compared to the current and cumulative emissions shown in Figure 8.1, this formula assigns a greater share of the global total to the developed countries: 34 percent to the US, 27 percent to the EU-27, and 8 percent to Japan; the total for high-income countries, including other industrial nations and high-income oil exporters, is 78 percent. China is responsible for 7 percent, and India for a mere 0.3 percent, of global costs.

Changes in income estimates would of course change these numbers. If it turns out that the previously published incomes for China and some other developing countries, used in the BAK calculations, have been overstated, then the same formula would shift even more of the global costs to high-income countries. On the other hand, China, India, and some other developing countries are currently growing faster than any of the high-income countries; if this trend continues, the greenhouse development rights formula will automatically shift more of the future responsibility onto the emerging economies as their incomes rise.

BAK propose that every country should begin by carrying out all of its own "no regrets" emissions reductions; their estimate of these opportunities is less optimistic than the figures discussed in Chapter 5. Since these reductions have no net cost, no one should get any credit for doing them. Then the cost-sharing formula, based on capacity and responsibility, should be used to allocate the (large) remaining reduction in emissions required for climate protection.

The costs that are being shared and the emissions that are being reduced are global, not national. It does not matter whether a country reduces a ton of carbon dioxide emissions at home or abroad; a ton of emissions reduction is equally valuable wherever it

occurs. Because the responsibility for reductions is based on historical emissions and on ability to pay, it is possible for a country to be
responsible for global reductions greater than its own current total
of emissions – and, indeed, the BAK formula implies that this is the
case for developed countries including the US, UK, and Germany.
In contrast, the responsibility of a country like China, with lower
historical emissions and limited ability to pay, is only enough to
slow the growth of its own emissions; in addition to China's own
efforts, other countries can discharge part of their responsibilities
by paying for reductions in China.

How much, in the end, will the global program of emissions
reduction cost? The Stern Review estimated that the total costs
of climate stabilization will amount to about 1 percent of world
output per year for some decades; the McKinsey studies discussed
in Chapter 5 came to similar conclusions. In that case, BAK's
greenhouse development rights formula implies annual costs per
"taxpayer" (i.e. per individual above the $9,000 poverty threshold)
of about $800 in the US, $400 in Japan and Europe, $140 in China,
and $50 in India. As noted above, the "taxpayers" who are above the
poverty line are a minority of the population in China and India,
but the great majority in the US, Europe, and Japan. The total
cost to the US, just over $200 billion per year, is comparable to
annual US military spending for the wars in Iraq and Afghanistan
as of 2007.[8]

All together now

International agreement is absolutely required to protect the climate.
No country alone accounts for more than about one-fifth of the
world's emissions; and carbon emissions affect everyone, regardless

of where they come from. We are all hostages to each other, with all of our futures depending on the goodwill of the rest of the world. Climate protection is essential but expensive; it will be tempting to be a "free rider," enjoying the benefits of everyone else's expenditures while not making any contribution of one's own. In order for an agreement to be adopted and carried out, it has to seem eminently fair to all concerned.

To be acceptable to developing countries, an agreement needs to have the developed countries bearing noticeably more of the global costs than their shares of current emissions. Both the cumulative history of emissions and the difference in economic resources to address the problem point toward rich countries paying more than in proportion to today's emissions. At the same time, an agreement must assign some responsibility for costs to China and other emerging economies, to address the complaints that kept the US out of the Kyoto Protocol.

Whether or not the details are correct, the greenhouse development rights proposal meets both requirements: the US, with 20 percent of current emissions, would pay 34 percent of the global costs; the corresponding figures for Europe are 14 percent of emissions and 27 percent of costs; and for Japan, 4 percent of emissions and 8 percent of costs. At the same time, the proposal judges people around the world by income rather than location, assigns some real responsibility to a country at China's level, and offers a transparent principle for gradually increasing a country's share of the global costs as its population moves out of poverty. Another formula for agreement could certainly be proposed, but it would have to meet roughly the same criteria to be accepted by both sides.

Cost–benefit analysis versus climate justice

There will, inevitably, be controversy about the next international agreement, concerning not only the details but also the underlying principles of equity. The conventional economic framework of cost–benefit analysis, discussed in earlier chapters, has little to say on issues of fairness: if a local environmental program could be financed, at the same total cost, either by taxing Bill Gates or by taxing the janitors in his office buildings, and the benefits would be the same in both cases, then there would be no obvious difference between the two alternatives from a cost–benefit perspective. The same is true for a global program of climate protection: if the total costs are the same, and the benefits are also the same, what is the difference in cost–benefit terms between the US and Europe paying for it on the one hand, or China and India on the other hand?

Along these lines, Eric Posner and Cass Sunstein, legal scholars who are among the leading advocates of cost–benefit analysis, have written a sweeping critique of the idea of climate justice.[9] While they agree that a new international agreement is needed, and that it might be desirable for the US to pay more in order to reduce costs in poor countries, they argue at length that there is no need to do so; they see no compelling moral principle which requires such generosity.

Posner and Sunstein view climate policy through the lens of cost–benefit analysis. Because the early stages of climate change will be less harmful to the US than to many other countries, they anticipate that the optimal policy for the US may be less ambitious than the solutions preferred by the rest of the world. They claim that the US is not obligated to spend more than its own interests would dictate, either on grounds of responsibility for past emissions ("corrective justice," in their terminology) or on the basis of its greater income and resources ("distributive justice").

Responsibility based on past emissions is not persuasive for Posner and Sunstein, even though those emissions still contribute to climate change. The past emissions occurred before many of the current residents of the US arrived in the country; they, and their ancestors, did not participate in the actions of "the country" over the past century. According to Posner and Sunstein, many of the residents of poor countries, the intended beneficiaries of climate programs, are not actually helpless victims – either because they are less at risk from climate change, or because they have the resources to protect themselves.

Responsibility based on unequal incomes is also said to be problematical. Posner and Sunstein argue that "significant greenhouse gas reductions are a crude and somewhat puzzling way of attempting to achieve redistributive goals."[10] It would be better, in their view, to decide how much to give to poor countries and then hand them the cash, to be spent as the recipients see fit, either on climate protection or on other goals. Even if both income redistribution and reduction of greenhouse gas emissions are separately desirable, Posner and Sunstein suggest that it is inefficient to try to achieve both goals at once in the same program.

Posner and Sunstein's objection to "distributive justice" claims, or responsibility based on past emissions, is largely answered by the greenhouse development rights proposal. Because it is based only on emissions since 1990, the proposal minimizes the problem of making recent immigrants responsible for events before they arrived. Most people in the US today either were here in 1990, or are the children of people who were here then. That relatively recent starting date also answers another objection: a century ago, no one could have been expected to know that their emissions were contributing to future climate problems. By 1990, the harm caused by carbon emissions was well known.

The objection to "corrective justice" claims, allocating responsibility based on ability to pay, is a familiar, unpersuasive one. Economics textbooks frequently discuss imaginary redistributions, or lump-sum transfers, divorced from all other issues, in order to separate considerations of income distribution from other aspects of economic policy. Often enough, the textbooks conclude that it is more efficient to address income distribution through lump-sum transfers, allowing other policy objectives to be pursued more directly.

In real life, such lump-sum transfers of income are rare and/or small events; there is little evidence of public support for redistribution of income per se, independent of context. Suggesting reliance on the fictitious social device of lump-sum transfers sounds, in practice, like a way to continue ignoring distributional questions. People may respond more strongly to concerns about equity when they are embedded in specific contexts such as climate policy, rather than presented as disembodied ethical principles.

Posner and Sunstein are among the most articulate advocates of conventional economic theory and cost–benefit analysis as guides to public policy; it is hard to see how that framework has helped to clarify their thoughts on climate change. If, as they say, they believe that redistribution of income and the creation of a new international climate agreement are both desirable, why argue at such length that there is no logical necessity for the US to do the right thing? Like the economic modelers discussed in earlier chapters, Posner and Sunstein have stretched traditional economic theories far beyond their limited domain of validity, resulting in unhelpful, misleading policy advice. Better approaches to climate economics are needed in order to develop better policies – the subject of the next, and final, chapter.

9

What is to be done?

The problem of climate change is too important to leave to the experts. A sustainable, low-emissions future must be built on a foundation of scientific and economic knowledge – but the challenge facing us is not only the development of new technologies. More immediately, we need to make much greater use of the technologies we already have. Our decisions about climate policy are, above all, ethical and political judgments about what we can and should do for each other today, and for the generations that will follow us.

The point of this book's journey through the economic debates is not just to explain the errors of conventional approaches and to outline a better theory. The larger goal is to inform the urgent and practical debate about climate policy – and to explain why the resolution of that debate will not emerge from economic modeling alone.

It may help to start with a summary of the argument so far. A widely publicized, conservative economic analysis recommends inaction on climate change, claiming that the costs currently out-weigh the benefits for anything more than the smallest steps toward reducing carbon emissions. This analysis is implicitly slanted in favor of the status quo, endorsing change only when the monetized value of benefits exceeds the costs of climate protection. The science of climate change, however, tells us that the status quo is not an available option for the future.

A better understanding of climate economics rests on the four "bumper stickers" introduced in Chapter 1.

Your grandchildren's lives are important   Climate change is a long-term problem, with impacts of current decisions extending over centuries to come. Any economic analysis over such spans of time is dominated by the choice of the discount rate, expressing our political and ethical judgments about the well-being of future generations. The judgment that the future matters to us today implies a low discount rate, which endorses a broad range of climate policy initiatives. In contrast, a high discount rate, whatever its justification, endorses doing almost nothing about climate policy.

We need to buy insurance for the planet   We don't know exactly how bad the earth's climate will get – and we don't know whether or when we will pass the tipping point for a catastrophic, irreversible event such as the loss of the Greenland ice sheet. The most likely outcomes of climate change look bad enough; the credible worst cases could involve the end of much of the human and other life on the planet. In this context, the details of the most likely outcomes are virtually irrelevant; all that matters is preventing the worst cases from occurring. These worst cases appear to be more likely than the individual losses for which people routinely buy insurance. Thus climate policy can be thought of as life insurance for the planet.

Climate damages are too valuable to have prices The cost–benefit approach stumbles when measuring and monetizing benefits; many of the most important benefits of climate protection are priceless. As a result, these benefits are either ignored or valued with incoherent, partial approximations for the purposes of cost–benefit calculations. To make these calculations complete and meaningful, it would be necessary to put prices on human lives, endangered species, ecosystems and much more. The attempts to invent such prices have produced ludicrous results.

Some costs are better than others On the other side of the ledger, orthodox economic theory exaggerates the costs of emissions reduction by rejecting the possibility of costless ("no-regrets") emissions savings, ignoring the jobs and incomes created by clean energy and efficiency expenditures, and assuming that the pace and direction of technological progress cannot be altered. In the imperfect real-world economy, the "good costs" of expenditures on climate mitigation are entirely preferable to the "bad costs" of physical damages caused by a worsening climate.

Turning toward policy solutions, the standard cost–benefit framework overlooks the question of equity. Some of the poorest countries of the world will be the first and hardest hit by the changing climate; they are among the least responsible for climate change, and the least able to pay for emissions reductions. Based on either historical emissions or current ability to pay, the developed countries should pay the bulk of the global costs of climate protection – in particular, they should pay more than their current share of worldwide emissions. Suppose, then, that a formerly recalcitrant country experiences a miraculous change of heart (or president) and steps forward to do its part to solve the global problem. What should it do?

Climate policy includes a complex mixture of technology, economics, and politics; a comprehensive account would require more than a single chapter or even a whole book. This chapter raises three last points about climate policy, three errors to avoid:

- Don't expect to find a simple technical fix – there are good reasons for skepticism about the leading proposals.
- Don't exaggerate the benefits of setting a price for carbon – market mechanisms may facilitate other policy changes, but will not solve the problem alone.
- Don't doubt that we can ultimately change fast enough – the first half of this century can, and must, see a total transformation in the way we produce and use energy.

Magic bullets that miss the target

Nothing is as appealing as the possibility of a technical solution, a breakthrough technology that could make the climate problem easy to solve. Unfortunately, three leading proposals for technical fixes have serious drawbacks.

Growing gasoline?   You can, it turns out, fuel your car with corn – more precisely, with ethanol derived from corn. Corn is a renewable resource; the carbon dioxide released when ethanol is burned will be reabsorbed when the next corn crop grows. The US has often produced more corn than the world wants to buy for feed and food; using the excess for fuel seems appealing, even to people who are not running for election in farm states.

Yet while corn itself is a renewable resource, additional energy is required to grow, harvest, and process the corn into ethanol; this energy comes from fossil fuels, resulting in carbon emissions. Some studies have found that the net energy balance is negative – the energy used to produce the ethanol is greater than the energy contained in the ethanol.[1] Perhaps a more common finding is that the balance is positive, but only slightly.[2] And although there's a lot of corn in the US, there's even more gasoline: turning the nation's entire corn crop into ethanol would replace only about one-fourth of gasoline use.[3]

The entire corn crop will never be poured into our gas tanks; long before that point, ethanol production would have intolerable effects on food prices and supplies. The ethanol boom has already driven up corn prices, raising the cost of living in countries such as Mexico where corn plays a major role in the diet.[4] As discussed in Chapter 4, the early stages of climate change will lower crop yields much sooner in tropical areas. Over at least the first half of this century, northern agricultural areas such as the US "Corn Belt" will account for an increasing fraction of the world's ability to produce food, while the population in developing countries will continue to grow. It is already problematic that we are feeding so much of the world's grain output to our cattle, rather than to people; the problem will be compounded if we also feed a lot of it to our cars.

Too cheap to meter, again?   Given the voracious appetite for electricity around the world, it will be essential to develop carbon-free sources of electric power. Nuclear power plants generate electricity from the fission of uranium atoms, a process that emits no carbon. Is it time to give this controversial technology another look? Expansion of nuclear power might someday be appropriate – but only if three seemingly intractable problems can be solved.

First, nuclear power, once touted as a source of electricity that would be too cheap to meter, has proved to be horrendously expensive, leading to bankruptcies and cancellations of partially built plants.[5] The expenses result in large part from the difficulty of making nuclear reactors safe; reducing costs by accepting higher risks of accidents would be a very bad bargain. Second, nuclear reactors require vast quantities of cooling water, which is hard to obtain during droughts and heat waves. The European heat wave of 2003 forced sharp reductions in the electrical output of nuclear plants, as did the drought in the southeastern US in 2007.[6] A different design would be needed to make nuclear power a robust technology for a warming world with frequent hot, dry spells. Finally, there is still no good plan for handling the nuclear waste from reactors, some of which remains dangerous for centuries or millennia. If the Roman Empire had had nuclear power, its waste sites would still be hazardous today. Our decisions about nuclear waste, like our decisions about climate change, will affect our descendants for many generations to come.

Cheap, safe, drought-resistant nuclear power, combined with a safe solution to the nuclear waste problem, would be widely welcomed – but it is not available, or even foreseeable, today. Waiting for a better nuclear option to emerge does not seem like a prudent response to the climate crisis.

Tinkering with the climate?   Geo-engineering solutions, intentionally modifying the climate, have been suggested at times, either out of technological hubris or political despair. Could we shoot something that would block or reflect incoming sunlight, such as sulfur particles or iron filings, into the upper atmosphere in order to reduce the amount of sunlight reaching the earth? There is an active, although worried and quite unresolved, discussion of this possibility among climate scientists.[7] Fine tuning would definitely be required; a little too much could launch a new ice age. Once started, an atmospheric shield that reduces global warming would have to be continuously maintained until carbon emissions have been lowered to a sustainable level; any failure of the shield could lead to extremely rapid warming, which could be worse than never having started.[8]

With climate change, we are struggling with the unintended, unforeseen consequences of past human activity; what would be the unintended consequences of shooting new materials into the skies? We have accidentally walked this way before: the rising use of coal in the second half of the twentieth century (before the 1980s in the US and other industrial countries, and more recently in China and India) led to growing levels of particulates in the atmosphere, slightly decreasing the intensity of sunlight reaching the earth and thereby slowing global warming.[9] Uncontrolled combustion of high-sulfur coal also led to acid rain, which kills forests, fish, and people more rapidly than the early stages of climate change. It was a big step forward for health and the environment when US sulfur emissions were regulated and acid rain was reduced.

The logic of carbon prices

Are market mechanisms and price incentives always the answer? Environmental advocates of an earlier generation would be surprised at the extent to which public policy, especially in the US, now takes for granted the centrality of the market. The high points of environmental improvement in the late twentieth century were achieved by the Clean Air Act, the Clean Water Act, and other laws that would now be disparaged as "command and control" regulation. In contrast, twenty-first-century climate policy seems sure to involve a leading role for either a carbon tax or a "cap and trade" system of tradable carbon emissions permits. Either one will result in a higher price for anything that causes carbon emissions, creating an incentive to seek alternatives with lower emissions.

The design of a carbon tax or trading system can make the distribution of income better or worse. Any carbon price will be regressive: it will take a larger percentage of income from lower-income people, effectively making the distribution of income more unequal.[10] This effect can be offset by the use of the revenue from a carbon tax. Equal per capita refunds for all, for example, would be progressive: this would boost incomes by a larger percentage among lower-income groups, making the distribution of income more equal. Refunds are not the only option; subsidies for energy efficiency improvements in low-income households would have a broadly similar effect.

A cap and trade system starts with a decision about the total allowable emissions per year, and then distributes permits or allowances to emit that amount. Since the allowances become a valuable new asset, it is important to watch how they are distributed. If the allowances are given away to current or past polluters, as happened with both the US system of sulfur emissions trading and the first version of the European trading system for carbon emissions, then industry receives a windfall, a gift of the newly created property. On the other hand, if emissions allowances are auctioned by the government, as called for in many newer proposals, then the revenues can be used for public purposes, exactly as with a carbon tax.

There are many more questions about the design of taxes and trading systems. International coordination between separate national policies will be needed; verification of reported emissions and reductions is a formidable challenge, especially when one country pays for reductions in another country. Sequestration – storing carbon in forests, soils, or other places that keep it out of the atmosphere – poses its own set of additional difficulties for record-keeping and verification.

The inefficiency of the market

Beyond such undeniably important issues about the design of market incentives, there is a larger question of what the market can and cannot achieve. As market-based policies become ever more intellectually fashionable, there is a danger of losing sight of their rationale, and their limitations.

This leads to one last excursion into economic theory: how do we know that reliance on the market is the right way to organize an economy? The most common answer to that question is obviously mistaken. The story of the invisible hand, the unconscious coordination of buyers and sellers through perfectly competitive markets that make everyone as well off as possible, is a fairy tale told by economists who should know better. As discussed in Chapter 1, the perfectly competitive equilibrium of the invisible hand story is clearly impossible in practice, and not even useful as a goal to strive toward.

The reasonable answer is a more modest claim: while not achieving the best of all possible worlds, the market does a credible job of decentralized processing of gigantic amounts of information – a task that no other system has proved capable of handling.

The market provides detailed, continuously updated information on what consumers want and what producers are offering. This is essential when, as is usually the case, there is great variation on one side of the market or the other: consumers want diverse and changing products, and companies have differing cost structures and production capabilities. Emissions trading can save money if some companies can reduce emissions more cheaply than others; trading then allows all the reductions to be done at the lowest-cost firms, rather than having to achieve equal reductions everywhere. On a grander scale, the centrally planned economy of the Soviet Union, the archetype of command-and-control organization, failed to produce the diverse and changing mix of goods that Soviet consumers wanted to buy as their incomes rose; in contrast, the market economy excels at solving this problem.

This story about the success of the market depends on the existence of variability. If all companies could reduce emissions at exactly the same cost, there would be no benefit to emissions trading; the total cost would be the same regardless of which firms did the reductions. If all consumers wanted the same, predictable goods and styles, there would be much less benefit from a competitive market for consumer products.

Uniformity among producers or consumers is not going to occur spontaneously. But something closely related does happen at times: if a society decides to mobilize all its resources for a single goal, the variation in individual objectives disappears – and so does the superior efficiency of the market. The mobilization for World War II is a case in point. Lester Brown has evoked the image of US wartime mobilization as a model for what needs to be done to address the environmental crisis;[11] in fact, the mobilization was impressive on both sides of the Atlantic. Soviet central planning, as bad as it was at meeting consumer demand in peacetime, was spectacularly good at rapidly shifting the nation's resources into military production – a fact that played no small part in determining the war's outcome.[12]

The war was not won by relying on free markets to make the crucial decisions. The US economy ran in a more planned, command-and-control mode during World War II than at any time before or since; automobile production was suspended for several years in order to produce more military vehicles, while gasoline and other goods were rationed. Would it have been more efficient for the Department of War, as it was then called, to compete with private consumers, paying so much for tanks and planes that the auto industry found it more profitable to produce them instead of cars? Or was it more efficient to pre-empt consumer demand so that industry could concentrate on meeting the singular national goal of the moment? When society's objectives are unitary, efficiency looks different, and the case for relying on price incentives looks weaker than in a "normally" diverse peacetime economy.

The implication for climate policy depends on how serious the problem has become. Does climate protection require the kind of total mobilization that was needed to win World War II? The Stern Review suggests as much, comparing the climate damages from business as usual to the effects of the world wars. Or is climate policy just one more brand competing in the marketplace against other initiatives, as Bjørn Lomborg and his "Copenhagen Consensus" assume? Stern clearly gets the better of this argument; the scientific warnings now seem to imply that we need a total mobilization to prevent dangerous climate change. In that context, continued reliance on market mechanisms may be justified as a consensus-building concession to those who do not yet share the sense of urgency, but it is not the way to achieve the best or fastest results. In short, market-based policies are a second-best, less efficient option for dealing with a threat to global survival, a compromise with political reality rather than a theoretical ideal.

Getting refrigerator prices right

Market incentives work better for some tasks than others; even in more mundane areas, it is worth exploring their limits as well as their strengths. Consider the problem of achieving energy efficiency in refrigerators, the largest use of electricity in many households. Refrigerators are available with widely varying energy use, for the same size and cooling power. For consumers with perfect information and foresight, higher energy prices provide a market incentive to buy more energy-efficient models; the refrigerator's lifetime energy cost will go up with higher carbon prices, making energy-saving models more attractive. Alternatively, regulations could require high and rising standards of energy efficiency for new refrigerators. (The US's minimum efficiency standards for refrigerators and other appliances are supposed to require the most energy-efficient level that is cost-effective for consumers; in practice, the standard-setting process often lags well behind the cost-effective frontier.[13])

The market-based option, giving consumers more choices and more information, is said by economic theorists to increase consumer welfare. How could it be bad to have more options? Yet relying on consumers to choose the more energy-efficient models requires either electricity prices so high that this factor dominates everyone's preferences, or an unlikely level of calculation and planning on those rare occasions when you are buying a fridge. Major appliance purchases occur so infrequently that few people develop much expertise in this field.

Even in theory, it may not be the case that more choices are always better. The overwhelming variety of consumer goods available in affluent economies can lead to what psychologist Barry Schwartz has described as the "paradox of choice": some amount of choice increases our sense of autonomy and freedom, but too much choice can lead to paralyzing indecision and anxiety about picking the wrong option.[14] How many refrigerator models do we need on the market in order to feel that we are free to choose? Are individual freedom and consumer satisfaction enhanced by allowing the sale of inefficient refrigerators that look deceptively cheap on the basis of purchase price, but are actually expensive if life-cycle energy costs are calculated correctly? Or do regulations requiring producers to make only high-efficiency models lighten the burden of comparison and decision-making for consumers?

In practice, for those who are looking for the most energy-efficient options, it can be frustratingly difficult to match the lists of efficient models to the specific choices available at local retail outlets. Energy efficiency is much less prominently advertised than size, price, color, and optional features; "big box" retail stores do not always carry the most efficient models. To achieve the maximum efficiency that is nominally available on the market today, different systems of information and distribution may be needed. That is, the effectiveness of market mechanisms may depend on the non-market policies and programs that accompany them.

Sulfur trading and why it works

Market mechanisms do not work in a vacuum; they are shaped by many other factors. The US system of sulfur emissions trading, the inspiration for many cap and trade proposals, is often credited with a dramatic reduction in the costs of pollution control. The Clean Air Act Amendments of 1990 established the system, setting a cap on sulfur emissions at about half of 1980 emissions and distributing allowances to businesses, roughly in proportion to past emissions. All large stationary sources of sulfur emissions, primarily coal-burning power plants, were included. The trading system was phased in from 1995 to 2000, with costs of controlling sulfur far below the levels that had been anticipated in advance.

However, this result is not attributable to trading alone; the low costs emerged quite early, at a time when the volume of emissions trading was still quite small.[15] Several other events also played important parts in driving down the costs. Just before trading began, a sharp reduction in railroad freight rates made it affordable to bring low-sulfur coal from Wyoming to Midwestern power plants, replacing high-sulfur coal from the closer Appalachian coal fields. Some state regulations required even more sulfur reduction than the national law, so it took no extra effort for power plants in those states to comply with the new national standard. At the same time, prices were declining for scrubbers, the pollution-control devices that remove sulfur emissions. In this context, the emissions trading system may have made some contribution to lowering costs, but it was playing on a field tilted in its favor. Without all the helpful coincidences, sulfur emissions trading would have looked much less successful.

If the US sulfur emissions trading experience is the model for carbon markets, then the most important question about market incentives may be, what other initiatives are needed to complement the market and again tilt the field in favor of success? It is not hard to identify the areas of energy efficiency, and low-carbon or no-carbon energy sources, where investment in research and development are needed. As seen in Chapter 5, this is not just a cost, but also an opportunity to create new industries and jobs, to launch a promising new path of technological development.

Can we change fast enough?

It is essential to adopt new climate policies at once, in order to address both the threat of crisis and the weight of inertia. In climate terms, carbon dioxide affects the climate for at least a century after it is emitted; and in economic terms, the investments that determine the level of emissions last for decades after they are built. Automobiles have a useful life of less than twenty years, which counts as the short run in climate calculations; a new generation of more fuel-efficient automobiles could replace old gas-guzzlers in the blink of a historical eye. Power plants last much longer, as do other buildings, including homes and settlement patterns in general.

One of the long-term problems to address is the trend toward suburban sprawl, which locks households into high uses of automobile transportation and creates a need for expensive, energy-inefficient housing and infrastructure. A low-carbon future requires more livable cities and less outer-ring suburban housing. The US should be trying to learn from the more energy-efficient European and Japanese urban models; at present, the opposite is unfortunately occurring, as the rest of the world is moving toward American-style, automobile-centered suburban living.

How realistic is it to expect that the world will shake off its inertia and act boldly and rapidly enough to make a difference? Projections from the latest IPCC reports, the Stern Review, and other sources suggest that it is still possible – if we start at once.

This may be the last generation that will have a real chance at protecting the earth's climate. If we spend twenty or thirty years talking about the need to get started and squabbling over shares of the costs, it will be all but impossible to avoid temperature increases that imply very dangerous climate risks.

There is a vast amount of upbeat news about small first steps being taken toward carbon reduction. Voluntary measures by businesses and non-profit organizations, and state and local government initiatives that have run far ahead of national policy in the US, are widely advertised today. On the one hand, these are indeed good news, testimony to both the extent of the no-regrets options for carbon reduction, and the initiative and concern of people everywhere. On the other hand, these are very small steps so far; it would be dangerous to conclude that continued voluntary efforts, perhaps combined with a small carbon price, could accomplish all of what is needed. Instead, these first steps should be used to build momentum for the larger and harder steps ahead.

A different kind of good news is suggested by the vast differences in per capita emissions among states in the US. Average CO_2 emissions in 2003 were around 20 tons per capita nationwide, but only 12 tons per capita in California and New York.[16] In contrast, emissions per capita reached 30 tons in Texas, and more than 60 tons in Alaska and Wyoming. On the one hand, every US state has higher per capita emissions than most other countries; the lowest is Vermont, at a little over 10 tons per capita. On the other hand, the wide disparity in US emissions levels suggests that a great deal could be accomplished just by bringing the entire country up to the level of best existing practices. If all of the US matched the performance of California and New York, the result would be a reduction of 40 percent of US emissions, or 8 percent of global emissions.

How do California and New York keep their per capita emissions 40 percent below the national average? In New York, the answer is largely the energy efficiency of life in New York City. Automobile use is at a minimum, and public transportation at a maximum, for the US; housing units are smaller than elsewhere in the country, and hence consume less energy, for the same level of income. This underscores the energy and emissions savings that can be achieved by combating suburban sprawl. However, New York City does not provide a model that can easily or quickly be adopted elsewhere.

California has a different pattern of emissions. Despite popular stereotypes about California's freeways and car culture, the state's per capita vehicle miles traveled and transportation emissions are essentially identical to the national averages. Most of the California difference in carbon emissions comes from the production and use of electricity. California's electricity is generated with much less coal, and more natural gas and renewable energy, than the US average. This remains true even when imports of electricity from other states are included (as they are in the 12 tons per capita emissions figure). In addition, Californians use less electricity per capita than the national average.

The state's cleaner fuel mix and lower electricity use are of roughly equal importance in holding emissions below the national average. Both factors result from decades of environmentally oriented state policy, driven in part by the need to reduce southern California's infamous air pollution. Today, California provides a large-scale, fully developed model of how to live comfortably with per capita carbon emissions 40 percent below the US average.

Needless to say, the state has achieved this lower emissions level using only existing, proven technology. If it were possible to adopt this model nationwide, the US could get halfway to the much-discussed goal of 80 percent emissions reduction by 2050, simply by having everyone live like Californians – an image that is not normally associated with hardship or deprivation.

Finally, consider even bigger pictures of the possibility of rapid economic and technological change. Cambridge University economist Ha-Joon Chang tells the (true) story of a developing country with a small, struggling automobile company that had been kept alive by government subsidies and trade protection.[17] In 1958 it attempted to export cars to the United States, and utterly failed, quickly withdrawing from the American market. Critics in the country's government argued, unsuccessfully, that this proved the country could never succeed in automobile production and should open its markets to cheaper foreign imports. The country was Japan, and the company was Toyota. At the time, Japan's per capita income was comparable to Argentina, and its leading export was silk.

The US and the world will have to travel well beyond California over the next fifty years, transforming the production and use of energy in order to build a low-carbon economy and protect the climate. Is the journey comparable to the distance from a silk-exporting developing country to twenty-first-century Japan? Rapid change has occurred, in Japan and elsewhere; no one ever has an accurate vision of the kind of industries and technologies that will exist fifty years in the future. Yet our actions today shape those future choices: the Japanese decision in 1958 to continue supporting Toyota, rather than embracing the short-run benefits of cheap American imports, had a momentous impact over the course of the next half-century.

Rapid change has occurred in the US as well. Fifty years ago, computers were enormous, expensive, and rare; the speculative science fiction of the day imagined that computers would only get bigger and bigger in the future. At about the same time, the US government, seeking to put a man on the moon and to invent a new arsenal of high-tech weaponry, was buying nearly all the production of transistors and integrated circuits (as discussed in Chapter 5) – technologies that eventually led to smaller and more powerful versions of computers, phones, and so much else. Microelectronics producers, like mid-twentieth-century Toyota, were at first hopelessly inefficient in free-market terms, and dependent on public support. The public-sector decisions to ignore short-run market calculations and continue supporting those industries made all the difference, creating the ubiquitous, advanced electronics that define so much of our economy today.

In a contemporary version of the same drama, which of today's clean energy initiatives will play the part of Toyota, or of the nascent microelectronics industry, soaring from "inefficient," government-subsidized beginnings to a force that leads and shapes the world market just a few decades later?

In the disaster movies described at the beginning of this book, as the fictional asteroid hurtles toward Earth, some combination of technology, hard work, and courage often succeeds in saving the planet. But not always.

Climate change is actually happening. This isn't a movie. Whether it's a disaster depends on what we all do next. A good first step is to throw out the misleading script written by conventional economics, which tells us to go slow. In its place, remember the four crucial principles from Chapter 1:

Your grandchildren's lives are important

We need to buy insurance for the planet

Climate damages are too valuable to have prices

Some costs are better than others

The real economics of climate change, based on these principles, shows that we can afford the future, after all.

Notes

Chapter 1

1. Nordhaus 2008, p. 15. His Figure 5.6, p. 102, suggests that "optimal" emissions in 2055 would be about one-third higher than in 2005.
2. Olmstead and Stavins 2006.
3. Baumol et al. 2006. Footnote 1 on page 1 lists the forty-two automobile dealers' associations that provided financial support.
4. This chapter draws heavily on Heinzerling and Ackerman 2007.
5. Above all, see the Fourth Assessment Report of the Intergovernmental Panel on Climate Change, available at www.ipcc.ch.
6. On the biases of cost–benefit analysis, see Ackerman and Heinzerling 2004; Ackerman 2008b.
7. Mas-Colell et al. 1995, p. 620.
8. On the resemblance of economics to physics, see Mirowski 1989; Ackerman 2002.
9. Friedman 1962, pp. 14–15.
10. Lipsey and Lancaster 1956.

Chapter 2

1. All compound interest and discounting examples in this chapter are based on annual compounding calculations. Compounding over a

different time period, or continuous-time calculation as in formal economic theory, would produce different numbers but would support the same qualitative conclusions.

2. All amounts of money greater than $1 have been rounded off to the nearest dollar.

3. 100-year numerical example used in Figures 2.1 and 2.2: benefits in year N, in billions of dollars, are arbitrarily set at $.06N^2$. The present value of a benefit B in year N, at a discount rate of r, is $B/(1+r)^N$.

4. For more detailed discussion see Ackerman 2007; Ackerman and Finlayson 2006. For citations to the academic literature on this topic, see those sources and the notes to Chapter 7.

5. Howarth 2003.

6. Ramsey 1928.

Chapter 3

1. In 2005 there were 511,000 fires in structures (US Census Bureau 2008, Table 346) and 124 million housing units in the US (US Census Bureau 2008, Table 953).

2. Based on US average death rates by age, as of 2004 (US Census Bureau 2008, Table 101).

3. LIMRA International, an insurance industry research group, reports that in families with dependent children, "Twenty-eight percent of wives and 15 percent of husbands have no life insurance at all. Ten percent of families with children under 18 have no life insurance protection." From "Facts About Life 2007," www.limra.com/press-room/pressmaterials/07USFAQ.pdf .

4. This is the so-called "Younger Dryas" period, when the dryas, today an alpine flower, can be found in fossils throughout Europe at low altitudes – suggesting that much colder conditions prevailed over a wide area. For an accessible entry into the extensive scientific literature (arguing for one of the possible triggers for the episode), see Broeker 2006.

5. The probability of *not* getting the highest of the 100 cards on one draw is 0.99. The probability of not getting it on any of N draws is 0.99^N. This probability is below 0.5 when N > 69, and below 0.05 when N > 299.

6. Weitzman 2007a, p. 9.

Chapter 4

1. Stanton and Ackerman 2007.

2. This section is based on Ackerman and Heinzerling 2004.

3. This account of methods of valuing life is based on Ackerman and Heinzerling 2004, pp. 75–84.
4. Among many other sources, see Ackerman and Heinzerling 2004, pp. 73–4.
5. Loomis and White 1996.
6. Kant 2005 [1785].
7. On the subjective enjoyment of warmer temperatures in Nordhaus's work, see Ackerman and Finlayson 2006.
8. Rehdanz and Maddison 2005.
9. Bosello et al. 2006.
10. Curreiro et al. 2002.
11. Ackerman and Stanton 2008a.
12. Deschenes and Greenstone 2007.
13. As recently as 2001, the national assessment by the US Global Change Research Program projected that the net impact of climate change on US agriculture would be positive throughout the 21st century (Reilly et al. 2001).
14. These are the Free-Air Carbon Dioxide Enrichment ("FACE") experiments – see IPCC 2007b, ch. 5.
15. Reilly et al. 2007.
16. Schlenker et al. 2006, studying agriculture east of the 100th meridian (almost none of which is irrigated).
17. Schlenker et al. 2007.

Chapter 5

1. The debate over the cost–benefit analysis of arsenic is discussed in Ackerman and Heinzerling 2004, pp. 91–3, 111–14.
2. IPCC 2007a, ch. 11.
3. Enkvist et al. 2007; Creyts et al. 2007.
4. McKinsey's US study assumed a long-run oil price of $59 per barrel; an increase of $25 above that level would have about the same effect as a carbon tax of $50 per ton of CO_2. That is, McKinsey's findings imply that an oil price of around $84 per barrel, with corresponding coal and gas price increases, would make it cost-effective to eliminate nearly one-third of US emissions. Predicting long-run oil prices is notoriously difficult, but as of mid-2008 the price remained well above $84 per barrel.
5. For a helpful theoretical treatment of this and many other issues in climate economics, see DeCanio 2003.

6. Wikipedia, "Amsterdam Airport Schiphol."
7. See the Apollo Alliance at www.apolloalliance.org. For related academic work on employment effects of clean energy options, see Pollin and Garrett-Peltier 2007; and other forthcoming work at www.peri.umass. edu.
8. Repetto and Austin 1997.
9. Nordhaus 2008, p. 166.
10. Abernathy and Wayne 1974.
11. Morton 1999.

Chapter 6

1. This chapter is excerpted from my review of *Cool It* (Ackerman 2008a).
2. Lomborg 2001.
3. Lomborg 2004.
4. Lomborg 2007, p. 159.
5. Ibid., p. 11.
6. Ibid., p. 169.
7. Ibid., p. 29.
8. Ibid., p. 174.
9. Ibid., p. 43.
10. Ackerman 2005.
11. Lomborg 2007, p. 37.
12. Ibid., p. 30.
13. Ibid., p. 31.
14. Ibid., p. 152.
15. Ibid., pp. 33–6.
16. Nordhaus and Boyer 1999.
17. Ibid., Table 6B. This is based on the more widely available 1998 draft of the manuscript which later appeared in the 1999 *Energy Journal* special issue.
18. Lasky 2003; Barker and Ekins 2004; Fischer and Morgenstern 2003.
19. Barker and Ekins 2004.

Chapter 7

1. Stern 2006.
2. This chapter is largely excerpted from the longer and more detailed treatment in Ackerman 2007.

3. Stern 2006, long executive summary, pp. 1–2.
4. Ibid., short executive summary, p. 1.
5. Unlike the US, the UK experienced heavy bombing during World War II. UK deaths, as a percentage of population, were three times the US level in World War II, and twenty times the US level in World War I (Wikipedia entries on "World War I casualties" and "World War II casualties").
6. Stern 2006, short executive summary, p. 1.
7. This includes estimates for the global warming impacts of methane and other greenhouse gases. The Stern calculations of CO_2-equivalent emissions include about 50 ppm contribution from non-CO_2 greenhouse gases; thus the range of 500–550 ppm of CO_2-equivalent emissions corresponds to 450–500 ppm of CO_2 alone.
8. This is comparable to 400–500 ppm of CO_2 alone (see previous note). The rationale for this target range is spelled out in chapter 13 of the Review, and discussed below.
9. Nordhaus 2007, p. 689.
10. Stern 2006, appendix to ch. 2, p. 48.
11. For a more detailed discussion of Nordhaus's approach to discount rates, see Ackerman and Finlayson 2006.
12. Dasgupta 2007.
13. Dietz et al. 2007.
14. Stern 2006, p. 153.
15. Baer 2007.
16. Weitzman 2007b.
17. Roughgarden and Schneider 1999.
18. Tol and Yohe, 2006, p. 236.
19. Mendelsohn 2006, p. 46.
20. Lomborg 2006.
21. Ackerman and Stanton 2008b.
22. Note that this is the mean PAGE model estimate as a percentage of US GDP in 2100; it is not directly comparable to the Stern Review's figures cited above for climate damages. The Stern Review calculated "balanced growth equivalents" for the entire stream of losses anticipated through 2200; a complex statistical process is required to reconcile balanced growth equivalents with losses expressed as a percentage of same-year GDP.
23. Maddison 2006, copy on file with author. Maddison's estimate for the growth of income appears to be a calculation of 194 years of compound growth at 1.3 percent, i.e. from 2006 to 2200.

24. Japan's real GDP growth averaged 3.9 percent per year from 1980 to 1990, then fell to 1.5 percent from 1990 to 2000. Calculated from Statistics Bureau, Ministry of Internal Affairs and Communication, *Historical Statistics of Japan*, www.stat.go.jp/data/chouki/zuhyou/03–21.xls. More recently, Japan's growth rate has risen, although not back to the 1980s' level.

Chapter 8

1. Many accounts of the Kyoto Protocol are available; the official website is http://unfccc.int/kyoto_protocol/items/2830.php.
2. See the literature on this subject reviewed in Ackerman et al. 2007, especially Ahmad and Wyckoff 2003.
3. Ackerman et al. 2007.
4. This discussion is based on data on historical and current emissions from the "Climate Analysis Indicators Tool (CAIT) Version 5.0" (Washington, DC: World Resources Institute, 2008), http://cait.wri.org/. The data include only CO_2 emissions from fossil fuel combustion and cement production.
5. Stott 2006.
6. Data on specific country emissions are from the World Resources Institute's CAIT (note 4 above), and from Baer et al. 2007.
7. Baer et al. 2007. All discussion here is based on the initial version, as published in late 2007. As this book went to press, a revision of the BAK calculations was under way, based in part on revised estimates of per capita incomes in some developing countries.
8. According to a Congressional Research Service report, "The Administration requested $195.5 billion for war-related activities for DOD, State/USAID and Department of Veterans' Affairs (VA) Medical for FY2008." Although a few smaller anti-terrorism programs were included, 95 percent of this proposed expenditure was for the wars in Iraq and Afghanistan. Amy Belasco, "The Cost of Iraq, Afghanistan, and Other Global War on Terror Operations Since 9/11," Congressional Research Service, 2008, p. i, www.fas.org/sgp/crs/natsec/RL33110.pdf.
9. Posner and Sunstein 2007, pp. 4, 36.
10. Ibid., p. 4.

Chapter 9

1. E.g. Pimentel and Patzek 2005.
2. Farrell et al. 2006. See also the critical letters and authors' response in *Science* 312(5781), 23 June 2006, pp. 1746–8.
3. Extrapolated from Westcott 2007, which reports that 14 percent of corn production in 2006 was used for ethanol, replacing 3.5 percent of gasoline use, and similarly projects that by 2017, 31 percent of corn will be used for ethanol, replacing 7.5 percent of gasoline use.
4. Sauser 2007.
5. Cohn 1997.
6. "Europe Swelters under Heat Wave," CNN.com, August 6, 2003, www.cnn.com/2003/WORLD/europe/08/05/heatwave/; J. Reeves, "Hot Weather Forces Partial Shutdown of TVA Nuclear Plant," *Associated Press*, 18 August 2007.
7. Morton 2007.
8. Brewer 2007.
9. Andreae et al. 2005.
10. A carbon price could be progressive in the lowest-income countries, since it imposes no costs on those who are too poor to buy commercial fuels. Among those who depend on commercial fuels, however, a carbon price is regressive, since lower-income groups spend a larger percentage of their incomes on energy. For empirical evidence on regressivity, see Wier et al. 2005.
11. Brown 2008.
12. Overy 1997, especially ch. 6.
13. American Council for an Energy-Efficient Economy, "Energy Department Grants Petition for New Refrigerator Energy Efficiency Standards," 13 April 2005, www.aceee.org/press/0504doepetition.htm.
14. Schwartz 2004.
15. Carlson et al. 2000; Ackerman and Moomaw 1997.
16. This discussion of state per capita emissions is based on Grubin 2008. Grubin used Energy Information Administration data for 2003 emissions, adjusted for interstate electricity trades based on Jiusto 2006, and personal communications from Dr. Jiusto.
17. Chang 2007, pp. 19–21.

References

Abernathy, W.J., and K. Wayne (1974). "Limits of the Learning Curve." *Harvard Business Review* 52(4): 109–19.

Ackerman, F. (2002). "Still Dead After All These Years: Interpreting the Failure of General Equilibrium Theory." *Journal of Economic Methodology* 9(2).

Ackerman, F. (2005). "Global Crises, Economists' Solutions?" *Journal of Industrial Ecology* 9(4): 249–52.

Ackerman, F. (2007). *Debating Climate Economics: The Stern Review vs. Its Critics*. www.ase.tufts.edu/gdae/Pubs/rp/SternDebateReport.pdf. Report for Friends of the Earth–England, Wales, and Northern Ireland.

Ackerman, F. (2008a). "Hot, It's Not: Reflections on *Cool It*, by Bjørn Lomborg." *Climatic Change* 89(3–4): 435–46.

Ackerman, F. (2008b). *Poisoned for Pennies: The Economics of Toxics and Precaution*. Washington DC: Island Press.

Ackerman, F., and I. Finlayson (2006). "The Economics of Inaction on Climate Change: A Sensitivity Analysis." *Climate Policy* 6(5).

Ackerman, F., and L. Heinzerling (2004). *Priceless: On Knowing the Price of Everything and the Value of Nothing*. New York: New Press.

Ackerman, F., M. Ishikawa and M. Suga (2007). "The Carbon Content of Japan–US Trade." *Energy Policy* 35(9): 4455–62.

Ackerman, F., and W. Moomaw (1997). "SO_2 Emissions Trading: Does It Work?" *Electricity Journal* 10(7): 61–6.

Ackerman, F., and E.A. Stanton (2008a). "A Comment on 'Economy-wide Estimates of the Implications of Climate Change: Human Health'." *Ecological Economics* 66(1): 8–13.

Ackerman, F., and E.A. Stanton (2008b). "The Cost of Climate Change: What We'll Pay if Global Warming Continues Unchecked." New York: Natural Resources Defense Council.

Ahmad, N., and A. Wyckoff (2003). *Carbon Dioxide Emissions Embodied in International Trade of Goods.* STI Working Paper 2003/15. Paris: OECD Directorate for Science, Technology and Industry.

Andreae, M.O., C.D. Jones and P.M. Cox (2005). "Strong Present-day Aerosol Cooling Implies a Hot Future." *Nature* 435: 1187–90.

Baer, P. (2007). "The Worth of an Ice-Sheet: A Critique of the Treatment of Catastrophic Impacts in the Stern Review." www.ecoequity.org/docs/WorthOfAnIceSheet.pdf.

Baer, P., T. Athanasiou and S. Kartha (2007). *The Right to Development in a Climate Constrained World.* Berlin, Heinrich Böll Foundation.

Barker, T., and P. Ekins (2004). "The Costs of Kyoto for the US Economy." *Energy Journal* 25(3): 53–71.

Baumol, W.J., R.W. Crandall, R.W. Hahn, P.L. Joskow, R.E. Litan and R.L. Schmalensee. (2006). "Regulating Emissions of Greenhouse Gases Under Section 202(a) of the Clean Air Act." www.aei-brookings.org/admin/authorpdfs/page.php?id=1336.

Bosello, F., R. Roson and R.S.J. Tol (2006). "Economy-wide Estimates of the Implications of Climate Change: Human Health." *Ecological Economics* 58(3): 579–591.

Brewer, P.G. (2007). "Evaluating a Technological Fix for Climate." *Proceedings of the National Academy of Sciences* 104(24): 9915–16.

Broeker, W.S. (2006). "Was the Younger Dryas Triggered by a Flood?" *Science* 312(5777): 1146–8.

Brown, L.R. (2008). *Plan B 3.0: Mobilizing to Save Civilization.* New York: W.W. Norton.

Carlson, C., D. Burtraw, M. Cropper and K.L. Palmer (2000). "Sulfur Dioxide Control by Electric Utilities: What Are the Gains from Trade?" *Journal of Political Economy* 108(6): 1292–1326.

Chang, H.-J. (2007). *Bad Samaritans: Rich Nations, Poor Policies, and the Threat to the Developing World.* London: Random House.

Cohn, S. (1997). *Too Cheap to Meter: An Economic and Philosophical Analysis of the Nuclear Dream.* Albany NY: State University of New York Press.

Creyts, J., A. Derkach, S. Nyquist, K. Ostrowski and J. Stephenson (2007). *Reducing U.S. Greenhouse Gas Emissions: How Much at What Cost?* New

York: The Conference Board, December.

Curriero, F.C., K.S. Heiner, J.M. Samet, S.L. Zeger, L. Strug and J.A. Patz (2002). "Temperature and Mortality in 11 Cities of the Eastern United States." *American Journal of Epidemiology* 155(1): 80–87.

Dasgupta, P. (2007). "Comments on the Stern Review's Economics of Climate Change (revised December 12, 2006)." *National Institute Economic Review* 199(1): 4–7.

DeCanio, S.J. (2003). *Economic Models of Climate Change: A Critique.* New York: Palgrave Macmillan.

Deschênes, O., and M. Greenstone (2007). *Climate Change, Mortality and Adaptation: Evidence from Annual Fluctuations in Weather in the U.S.* Department of Economics Working Papers. Cambridge MA: MIT.

Dietz, S., C. Hope, N. Stern and D. Zenghelis (2007). "Reflections on the Stern Review (1): A Robust Case for Strong Action to Reduce the Risks of Climate Change." *World Economics* 8(1): 121–68.

Enkvist, P.-A., T. Nauclér and J. Rosander (2007). "A Cost Curve for Greenhouse Gas Reduction." *The McKinsey Quarterly* 1 (February): 35–45.

Farrell, A.E., R.J. Plevin, B.T. Turner, A.D. Jones, M. O'Hare and D.M. Kammen (2006). "Ethanol Can Contribute to Energy and Environmental Goals." *Science* 311(5760): 506–8.

Fischer, C., and R. Morgenstern (2005). "Carbon Abatement Costs: Why the Wide Range of Estimates?" Washington DC: Resources for the Future, Discussion Paper 03–42.

Friedman, M. (1962). *Capitalism and Freedom.* Chicago: University of Chicago Press.

Grubin, E.S. (2008). "Reducing Per Capita Emissions: California as a Climate Change Policy Role Model or Rebel?" Master's thesis. Department of Urban and Environmental Policy and Planning, Tufts University.

Heinzerling, L., and F. Ackerman (2007). "Law and Economics for a Warming World." *Harvard Law and Policy Review* 1(2): 331–62.

Howarth, R. (2003). "Discounting and Uncertainty in Climate Change Policy Analysis." *Land Economics* 79(3): 369–81.

Intergovernmental Panel on Climate Change (2007a). *Climate Change 2007: Mitigation of Climate Change. Contribution of Working Group III to the Fourth Assessment Report of the Intergovernmental Panel on Climate Change.* Cambridge: Cambridge University Press.

Intergovernmental Panel on Climate Change (2007b). *Climate Change 2007: Summary for Policy Makers. Contribution of Working Group II to the Fourth Assessment Report of the Intergovernmental Panel on Climate Change.* Cambridge: Cambridge University Press.

Jiusto, S. (2006). "The Differences that Methods Make: Cross-border Power Flows and Accounting for Carbon Emissions from Electricity Use." *Energy Policy* 34(17): 2915–28.

Kant, I. (2005) [1785]. *Groundwork for the Metaphysics of Morals (Grundlegung zur Metaphysik der Sitten)*, trans. Thomas K. Abbott; with revisions by Lara Denis, ed. Lara Denis. Orchard Park NY: Broadview Press.

Lasky, M. (2003). "The Economic Costs of Reducing Emissions of Greenhouse Gases: A Survey of Economic Models." Washington DC: Congressional Budget Office, Technical Paper Series 2003–3.

Lipsey, R.G., and K. Lancaster (1956). "The General Theory of Second Best." *Review of Economic Studies* 24: 11.

Lomborg, B. (2001). *The Skeptical Environmentalist: Measuring the Real State of the World*. Cambridge: Cambridge University Press.

Lomborg, B., ed. (2004). *Global Crises, Global Solutions*. Cambridge: Cambridge University Press.

Lomborg, B. (2006). "Stern Review: The Dodgy Numbers behind the Latest Warming Scare." *Wall Street Journal*, 2 November.

Lomborg, B. (2007). *Cool It: The Skeptical Environmentalist's Guide to Global Warming*. New York: Alfred A. Knopf.

Loomis, J.B., and D.S. White (1996). "Economic Benefits of Rare and Endangered Species: Summary and Meta-analysis." *Ecological Economics* 18(3): 197–206.

Maddison, D. (2006). "Further Comments on the Stern Review." www.economics.bham.ac.uk/maddison/Stern%20Comments.pdf.

Mas-Colell, A., M. Whinston and J. Green (1995). *Microeconomic Theory*. New York: Oxford University Press.

Mendelsohn, R.O. (2006). "A Critique of the Stern Report." *Regulation* 29(4): 42–6.

Mirowski, P. (1989). *More Heat than Light: Economics as Social Physics, Physics as Nature's Economics*. New York: Cambridge University Press.

Morton, D. (1999). "The Electrical Century: What Difference Did Semiconductors and Microelectronics Make?" *Proceedings of the IEEE* 87(6): 1049–52.

Morton, O. (2007). "Is This What It Takes to Save the World?" *Nature* 447: 132–6.

Nordhaus, W.D. (2007). "A Review of *The Stern Review on the Economics of Climate Change*." *Journal of Economic Literature* 45(3): 17.

Nordhaus, W.D. (2008). *A Question of Balance: Economic Modeling of Global Warming*. New Haven: Yale University Press.

Nordhaus, W.D., and J. Boyer (1999). "Requiem for Kyoto: An Economic

Analysis of the Costs of the Kyoto Protocol." special issue on Kyoto, *Energy Journal* 20: 93–130.

Olmstead, S., and R. Stavins (2006). "An International Policy Architecture for the Post-Kyoto Era." *American Economic Review* 96(2): 35–8.

Overy, R. (1997). *Why the Allies Won.* New York, W.W. Norton.

Pimentel, D., and T.W. Patzek (2005). "Ethanol Production Using Corn, Switchgrass, and Wood; Biodiesel Production Using Soybean and Sunflower." *Natural Resources Research* 14(1): 65–76.

Pollin, R., and H. Garrett-Peltier (2007). *The U.S. Employment Effects of Military and Domestic Spending Priorities.* Amherst, Working paper 152, Political Economy Research Institute, University of Massachusetts, www.peri.umass.edu.

Posner, E.A., and C. Sunstein (2007). "Climate Change Justice." University of Chicago Law and Economics Olin Working Paper No. 354 (August).

Ramsey, F.P. (1928). "A Mathematical Theory of Saving." *The Economic Journal* 138(152): 543–59.

Rehdanz, K., and D. Maddison (2005). "Climate and Happiness." *Ecological Economics* 52: 111–125.

Reilly, J.M., J. Graham and J. Hrubovcak (2001). *Agriculture: The Potential Consequences of Climate Variability and Change for the United States.* US Global Change Research Program, New York: Cambridge University Press.

Reilly, J., S. Paltsev, B. Felzer, X. Wang, D. Kicklighter, J. Melillo, R. Prinn, M. Sarofim, A. Sokolov and C. Wang (2007). "Global Economic Effects of Changes in Crops, Pasture, and Forests due to Changing Climate, Carbon Dioxide, and Ozone." *Energy Policy* 35(11): 5370–83.

Repetto, R., and D. Austin (1997). *The Costs of Climate Protection: A Guide for the Perplexed.* Washington DC: World Resources Institute.

Roughgarden, T., and S. Schneider (1999). "Climate Change Policy: Quantifying Uncertainties for Damages and Optimal Carbon Taxes." *Energy Policy* 27: 415–29.

Sauser, B. (2007). "Ethanol Demand Threatens Food Prices." *Technology Review.* www.technologyreview.com/energy/18173.

Schlenker, W., W.M. Hanemann and A.C. Fisher (2006). "The Impact of Global Warming on U.S. Agriculture: An Econometric Analysis of Optimal Growing Conditions." *Review of Economics and Statistics* 88(1).

Schlenker, W., W.M. Hanemann and A.C. Fisher (2007). "Water Availability, Degree Days, and the Potential Impact of Climate Change on Irrigated Agriculture in California." *Climatic Change* 81: 19–38.

Schwartz, B. (2004). *The Paradox of Choice: Why More is Less.* New York, HarperCollins.

Stanton, E.A., and F. Ackerman (2007). *Florida and Climate Change: The Costs of Inaction.* Global Development and Environment Institute and Stockholm Environment Institute US Center, Medford MA: Tufts University.

Stern, N. (2006). *The Stern Review: The Economics of Climate Change.* London, HM Treasury.

Stott, R. (2006). "Contraction and Convergence: Healthy Response to Climate Change." *British Medical Journal* 332: 1385–7.

Tol, R.S.J., and G.W. Yohe (2006). "A Review of the Stern Review." *World Economics* 7(4): 233–50.

US Census Bureau. (2008) "Statistical Abstract of the United States." 127th edition, www.census.gov/statab/www/.

Weitzman, M.L. (2007a). "On Modeling and Interpreting the Economics of Catastrophic Climate Change (December 5, 2007 version)." www.economics.harvard.edu/faculty/weitzman/files/modeling.pdf.

Weitzman, M.L. (2007b). "A Review of the Stern Review on the Economics of Climate Change." *Journal of Economic Literature* 45(3): 703–24.

Westcott, P.C. (2007). *Ethanol Expansion in the United States: How Will the Agricultural Sector Adjust.* U.S. Department of Agriculture, Economic Research Service. www.ers.usda.gov/Publications/FDS/2007/05May/FDS07D01/fds07D01.pdf

Wier, M., K. Birr-Pedersen, H.K. Jacobsen and J. Klok (2005). "Are CO_2 Taxes Regressive? Evidence from the Danish Experience." *Ecological Economics* 52(2): 239–251.

All websites current as of January 2008.

Index

ability to pay, 107, 111, 115
acid rain, 119
AEI–Brookings think-tank, 3
Afghanistan, US military spending, 107
agriculture, 12; carbon dioxide fertilization, 52; global regions, 53; northern, 49; warming impacts, 51
AIDS prevention, cost–benefit analysis, 77
air pollutants, 46
Airbus, 10
Alaska, high per capita emissions, 128
Apollo Alliance, 63
Argentina, emissions level, 103
Athanasiou, Tom, 104; BAK proposal, 105
Australia, carbon exporter, 99
"autonomous energy efficiency improvement," 65

Baer, Paul, 89–90, 92–3, 104; BAK proposal, 105–7
BAK (Baer, Athanasiou and Kartha) proposal: individual incomes basis, 105; cost-sharing formula, 106–7
Belarus, emissions level, 103
Boeing, 10
Brazil: average income, 105; emissions level, 103
Brown, Gordon, 82
Brown, Lester, 122
buildings, energy efficiency/inefficiency, 59–60
Bulgaria, average income, 105
Bush, G.W., 45

California, low per capita emissions, 128–30
Cambridge University, 93, 130
Canada, carbon exporter, 99
carbon: prices, 116, 119; soil and forest sequestration, 35; taxes, 2, 57, 73–4, 81

international trade, pollution impact,
99
Internet, ARPANET origins, 68
Iraq: US military spending, 107; US
soldier death likelihood, 31
Ishikawa, Masanobu, 100

Japan: BAK implications, 106; carbon
importer, 99; consumption
responsibility, 100; cumulative
emissions, 101; lost decade of
economic growth, 94–5; per
capita emissions, 103; poverty
numbers, 105; reduction costs
responsibilities, 108; urban model,
127
job creation, municipal politics,
64

Kant, Immanuel, 48
Kartha, Sivan, 104; BAK proposal,
105
Keynes, John Maynard, 11, 63–4
Kobe University, 100
Kyoto Protocol, 2, 72; "common but
differentiated responsibilities," 97;
Annex I, 98–9; costs
misrepresentation, 80–81; US
non-ratification, 108

laissez-faire policies, 9
Lancaster, Kelvin, 10
levee building, economic
consequences, 61
life-year calculations, age bias, 46
Lipsey, Richard, 10
Lomborg, Bjørn, 50, 70–71, 91, 123;
assumptions of, 78; authority
claim, 72; errors, 73; false choices
presentation, 77; Kyoto costs
misrepresentation, 81; media
attention, 4; sources bias, 74–5,
80; Stern Review criticism, 79;
wishful thinking of, 76

lump-sum redistributive transfers,
fictitious notion, 111

Maddison, David, 94
major war, monetary estimate
inadequacy, 95
Malthus, Thomas, 11–12
market, theories of, *see* competitive
markets
market-based policies: incentives
limits, 124, 126; wider limitations,
121
Marx, Karl, 11
McKinsey & Co., 57; emissions
study, 58, 107
Mendelsohn, Robert, 91
methane, 34
Mexico: corn price rise, 117;
emissions level, 103
Miami: sea-level rise consequences,
44; temperature, 51
microelectronics industry, initial US
government support, 67–8, 131
Microsoft, software dominance, 10
MIT (Massachusetts Institute of
Technology), 3
moderate warming, benefit claims,
48–9, 91
Monte Carlo analysis, 89–90
municipal politicians, job creation
interest, 64

NASA, scientists, 1
Netherlands, rising sea protection, 62
New Orleans: destruction of, 62;
temperature, 49
New York, low per capita emissions,
128–9
Nigeria, emissions level, 103
Nordhaus, William, 2, 49–50, 66, 78,
80, 85–6, 89–90
nuclear power, 117; waste problem
longevity, 118
numbers, sociology of, 42